Praise for *Forgiveness Dies*

"Is someone setting Trevor Galloway up, or is his own mind deceiving him? *Forgiveness Dies* puts a uniquely fascinating protagonist—a detective who can't trust his own perceptions—into a complex political thriller, and the result is propulsive. Hensley starts with a punch, and accelerates from there."

—Joseph Finder,
New York Times bestselling author

"Inventive storytelling meets propulsive action in this wild thrill ride from J.J. Hensley, who brings real-life experiences to the page and delivers an authentic tale of double-crosses and dirty dealings. Don't worry if you haven't stepped into Trevor Galloway's shadowy world yet...start right here, and you'll soon want to read them all!"

—Daniel Palmer,
USA Today bestselling author

"*Forgiveness Dies* is a non-stop, gut churning thriller that you'll read in one sitting. Hensley has conceived a brilliant but almost fatally flawed protagonist in Trevor Galloway, a man so tormented by his past that in the battle for truth and justice he's forced to fight enemies that are dangerously real, and some that only real to him. J.J. Hensley is one of the best thriller writers out there, and he sits at the top of my must-read list."

—Mark Pryor,
author of the Hugo Marston series

FORGIVENESS DIES

J.J. HENSLEY

FORGIVENESS DIES

A Trevor Galloway Thriller

DOWN&OUT
BOOKS

Down & Out Books
3959 Van Dyke Road, Suite 265
Lutz, FL 33558
DownAndOutBooks.com

Cover design by JT Lindroos

ISBN: 1-64396-038-5
ISBN-13: 978-1-64396-038-8

To Kasia and Cassie

PROLOGUE

Pittsburgh

There is no recovering from an amputated heart. There is no cure for total loss. You can replace what has been taken, attempt to fill the void, and mitigate your own culpability. The symptoms can be treated, the rage may be quelled, the sharp edges of the memories can be dulled with pills that slide down your throat with the gentlest push, but the underlying cavity in one's being aches to be filled with what can never be returned. It's been over three years, but my home is as it was when I left. When I was taken. When everything important to me was taken.

"I tried to keep things in decent order," said Chase as he flicked on some lights.

I nodded and set my bag on the floor.

"You'll need groceries," he said. "We can order in tonight and then I'll take you shopping in the morning."

The air in the house wasn't stagnant. He'd been inside recently and opened the windows. It occurred to me the lights coming on meant the utilities had been paid.

"Did you pay my bills?" I asked.

Chase hesitated and became visibly uncomfortable. He was handling me with kid gloves and I couldn't blame him. The state said I could leave the institution, but that didn't mean I was well. I wasn't well. I couldn't see *well* with a telescope.

He shrugged and said, "When I knew you weren't coming

back for a while, I had your utilities paid automatically from your bank account. I didn't know for sure when you were getting out, so it didn't make sense to shut them off in case the doctors suddenly signed off on your release."

Something about what he said seemed familiar, but I wasn't sure why.

I said, "I couldn't have had enough in my account to keep up the payments."

Chase watched me as if he wasn't sure I was being serious. When an appropriate amount of time passed so that he understood my apparent lack of understanding was real, he said, "You had some money coming to you from your last case. Those funds covered your bills and then some. You still have some money in your checking account, but only enough to last you for a few months. Of course, you are still getting your disability pension from the department, but that's not exactly lottery money."

There it was again—the familiarity. Then, it hit me.

"We've discussed this, haven't we?"

Chase broke off eye contact and looked at the floor.

"How many times?" I asked.

His eyes came up and he answered, "A few. We worked with the bank to set it all up."

"I'm sorry," I said.

Chase shook his head. "I'm the one who's sorry. I wish I could have done more for you."

"You did plenty," I told him.

"I'm a cop," he said. "I should have...if I would have..."

"I killed people, Chase. I killed a lot of people."

He squeezed his mammoth hands into the pockets of jeans and said, "You had every reason to do what you did. Besides, you weren't in your right mind at the time. At least the court got that part right. I'm sure being locked away in a psych hospital was no picnic, but prison would have been worse."

He was right. And he was wrong.

A long moment stretched out with neither of us speaking. At

least, I think it was a long pause. Maybe the moment was only a second. While my treatment had helped me maintain a better grasp on what was real, I had become woefully inept when it came to gauging the passing of time. I glanced around the living room and saw my television, my bookshelf, and finally a turntable in the corner. The same record I'd been playing at the time of my arrest sat on the turntable, untouched as I knew it would be. My gaze settled on it and I wondered if the meds they gave me would continue to hold or if fantasy would creep back into reality.

"Is pizza okay?" he asked.

A certificate hung on the wall above the dusty record. Inside the frame was a commendation I'd received from the Pittsburgh Bureau of Police for outstanding work on a narcotics investigation. According to the document behind the glass, Detective Trevor Galloway had *demonstrated outstanding valor in the performance of his duties and completed work instrumental to the disruption of illegal drug activities in Pittsburgh.*

A lifetime ago.

A life before I'd been forced to battle my own addiction to heroin, then pills, and finally had to deal with an assortment of hallucinations. The meds I'd been prescribed had eliminated the hallucinations, but rendered me all but useless when it came to engaging in any activity requiring analytic ability. When properly medicated, I was fairly sane, but as insightful as a stapler. Throughout the time I'd worked as a private investigator—albeit unlicensed—I had a history of wandering off my meds long enough to work a case. Thus far, that strategy had not worked out particularly well.

"Trevor?"

"What?" I asked, turning back to Chase.

He frowned. "Is pizza okay?"

"Oh. Sure," I replied while looking back toward the certificate.

"Hey."

I looked at my friend and saw the concern on his face. Realizing what he must be thinking, I said, "I'm not seeing anybody. I'm just looking around the room."

His expression was skeptical, but he pulled his cell phone out to order the pizza.

"I promise," I said while he was dialing. "Go ahead and order for the three of us."

He froze mid-dial and stared me down. With no effort, I was able to keep my serious expression chiseled in stone. It was a mannerism that had helped me acquire an unfortunate nickname that Chase loved to use. After a few beats, I decided to let him off the hook.

"I'm kidding," I assured him.

He grimaced and took in a deep breath before speaking. "You're a riot. The Tin Man has a funny bone. Who knew?"

I knew I wasn't really funny. I also knew what was still lying underneath my stoicism and reassuring comments. I knew something I couldn't tell anybody. Chase, like everyone else, thought I had suffered a psychological break when I had killed those men. How had he phrased it? *I wasn't in my right mind at the time.*

My lawyer had spun the story and the shrinks had bought into the tale after a series of interviews and tests. But, I knew the truth. Regardless of what the legal system had determined, I had known what I was doing. Many things had gone off the rails that day, but my mind was not one of them.

In the three weeks since Chase had brought me home, I'd left my house exactly three times. Through the haze of my medications, I'd managed somehow to economize my outings in order to get my driver's license renewed, get my car inspected and road ready, shop for groceries, and meet with my court-appointed therapist. I'd spent most of the other days watching television in my living room while battling the eternal drowsiness produced by the battery of pills that tethered me to reality and kept the volume of my suicidal thoughts to a minimal decibel level. Chase stopped by every few days and did his best to mask his concerns while prodding me to reenter a society that didn't want me as a member. His efforts to push me forward would lose traction as he came to realize that neither of us had any idea what my reintroduction to the world would entail. My days as a cop were long gone. My attempts at being a private investigator had ended disastrously. Finding a potential employer that wouldn't set fire to a resume that included being invited to leave the profession of law enforcement, having committed multiple homicides, while advertising a stunning absence of marketable skills, would be challenging. Aside from Chase, my best personal references were hallucinations I hadn't seen in a while and even some of those hated me. Not an ideal situation.

December's idleness turned to loathing and self-pity in January. As the sun struggled to hang in the sky a little longer each evening, I began to dread the coming months when I'd look out my window to see others in my Brookline neighborhood buzzing around with activity as I wasted time watching political analysts dissect an election still nearly two years away. If not for my laziness, I probably would have started using heroin again or at least poured enough alcohol down my throat to obliterate a few more memories. Instead I sat as life slowly rolled by. Then in week four—or was it five or six—the doorbell rang.

"Trevor," said the man after he assessed my appearance through the gap in the partially open door. "It's been a long time."

I nodded and rubbed the stubble on my face.

"It's kind of cold out here," he said.

I tried to say something to agree with him, but since I hadn't used my voice for quite some time the words got caught in my throat.

"Trevor," he said again. "It's cold. Can I come inside?"

"Oh, yeah," I managed to say as I pulled the door wide open.

I took a step back and watched Nick Van Metre enter and

appraise his surroundings. Apparently finding nothing in my living room to be of particular interest, his attention turned back to me. I closed the door behind him.

"You don't look well," he observed.

I looked down at my sweatpants and torn sweatshirt. I wasn't wearing shoes and the top of one of my white socks had a stain from some coffee I'd spilled.

"Laundry day," I said truthfully. Of course, it had been laundry day for the past four days and I simply hadn't gotten around to doing any.

"You're pale. Have you been eating?"

"Are you here to hurt me?"

He seemed to be taken aback by the question, delayed, but then answered, "No, Trevor. I don't blame you for the way things went down. You interfered with an official Secret Service investigation, but what happened wasn't your fault."

Now it was my turn to wordlessly size him up. He must have sensed my skepticism, so he continued.

"Yes, at first I was angry with you. You had been told to stay out of the way of a major counterfeiting investigation and you did the opposite. But, I understand why you did what you did and once Jackie got hurt..." Emotion showed in Nick's face as he remembered his partner. "Once she got hurt, you took care of business in a way none of our agents could have. You did what all of us wanted to do."

Memories I had been trying to suppress were pushing their way to the surface. An uncomfortable silence descended upon us until I said, "Not everybody in your agency felt the same."

"You know how it works," said Nick. "For the sake of appearances, they had to denounce you in public. But privately, you had a lot of support."

I wasn't sure I believed him, but it wasn't an issue worth debating.

"Did something else happen with that case?" I asked.

"It wrapped up a long time ago," he said. "Why do you ask?"

"Because you're here."

His brown hair was longer than I remembered. He raised his hand and moved several strands off his forehead before gesturing to a couple of chairs. "Can we sit?"

Nick removed his coat, hung it over the back of a chair and took a seat. I maneuvered the matching IKEA purchase opposite him and observed his muscular physique. I'd been in fairly good shape when we'd first met. Now, I was thinner than I'd been since college and had the muscle tone of a long-term coma patient. I'd tried exercising in the institution and again upon my release, but the meds that disrupted the gravitational pull causing insane visions to orbit me also depleted my energy and motivation. Nick's fitness made me self-conscious of my own frailty and I hopelessly adjusted my posture in a feeble attempt to feel adequate.

"I'm not with the Secret Service anymore," he told me.

He was still young and nowhere near retirement age, so the appropriate thing was for me to have asked why he left. I could guess it had something to do with the emotional fallout from the case I had gotten involved with, so I chose to keep my mouth shut and not ask about his motivation.

"What do you do for a living?" I heard myself say.

My mind immediately drifted to the series of events that had gotten me arrested. I saw the flashes of the things I'd done. It was a miracle that I hadn't ended up dodging shanks in general population rather than attending mandatory therapy sessions and swallowing little round tablets of serenity. My recollections from the institution already seemed more like dreams than actual memories. The passage of time had blurred the faces of doctors whose names I had already forgotten. I was doing my best to remember the instructions I had been given. Always take the meds at the right times. Get fresh air and exercise. Focus on the future rather than the past. Avoid stress.

"That's where you come in," Nick said.

I opened my mouth, but had nothing to say.

He asked, "What do you think?"

Nothing. I'd heard nothing of what he'd been explaining. What was the last thing I remembered? What had I asked him?

"I'm sorry, Nick. The medication I take makes it difficult for me to focus. I think you were telling me you weren't with the Secret Service anymore, right?"

His face fell and even with my limited powers of observation I could read his discouragement. He resigned himself to begin again, but I sensed he was having second thoughts about speaking to me at all.

"I work for a company called Metal Security. We investigate corporate fraud, handle employment background investigations, and provide executive security. I supervise the Executive Security branch, which handles protection for some high-profile individuals in Fortune 500 companies. One of those individuals is Pittsburgh's own Dennis Hackney. I assume you know the name."

I did, thanks to the hours I'd been spending watching political shows on the news channels.

"He says he's running for president," I said, relieved that I knew anything at all. A feeling of pride swelled within me, and then shame that I felt proud about knowing something everyone else in the country knew. Then I remembered what else I knew from the broadcasts I'd viewed. I said, "He pisses people off."

Nick smiled. "He does do that. Between the two of us, he's a dick. Even worse, he's a zealot, a bigot, and believes God has chosen him to weed out the *undesirable* components of society. But, he pays Metal Security to protect him and they pay me. So here we are."

Here we were. Yet, I had no idea why "we" involved "me." I held my hands out apologetically and said, "You probably told me a minute ago, but can you explain to me why you are telling me all this?"

Nick said, "I figure we are still a few months away from Hackney making a request for Secret Service protection. He'll be considered a major candidate, so I have no doubt that the request will be approved and the agency will take over. At which point, my guys will either discontinue operations or be relegated to working as little more than event staff. Until then, Hackney is my responsibility. As you mentioned, he's angered a lot of people and made some enemies. Lately, one person in particular, using the name 'Chaerea,' emailed a threat to his website."

"Chaerea? That's an odd word. Is that a place? Something mythological?" I asked.

"It's not a what, but a who," said Nick. "The chosen screen name is one reason I'm concerned. The name Chaerea is likely a reference to the Roman Cassius Chaerea who assassinated Emperor Caligula. Caligula thought himself to be a god. Chaerea proved him wrong."

"So, your suspect knows a little history," I said.

"It would seem so. Or maybe it's just some nutcase who likes to read entries on Wikipedia or perhaps it's a local college student studying ancient Rome."

"Local?" I asked.

Nick nodded. "The IP address attached to the message is local, but not a residence. Normally, I wouldn't worry about something like this since the truly dangerous ones typically don't invite attention by making threats. However, these messages have me concerned. Hackney is about to crank up his number of public appearances as he makes a run toward the primary elections. The publicity is going to be something fierce. Recently, it's become known that out of all the companies Hackney runs, every single board member is white. That has the potential of becoming a big story."

"All of them?" I asked.

"Well, now they are," Nick replied. "A Hispanic man named Hector Solis was on the board of Hackney's investment bank, but died in a hit-and-run last year." Nick rolled his eyes. "That investment bank may be another powder keg as well." He waved off the thoughts of the aggravations to come. "Anyway, the campaign strategy has him starting here in Pennsylvania and then branching out to the rust belt states. Hackney is calling it the 'Knock the Rust Off Tour.' He, and his wife Alana, who is almost always with him, will be hitting a ton of spots nationally. That information isn't public, but the person making the threats knew about it in advance. He or she even used the name of the tour." Nick folded leaned forward and folded his hands in front of him. "I want to hire you to find and identify Chaerea."

I thought I must have gotten my meds mixed up.

"Excuse me?"

"I could use your help," he said.

I waited for a punchline that never came.

"Nick, I just got out of a mental institution because I murdered people. I'm a recovering drug addict who was forced out of police work. If untreated, I have hallucinations. At this very moment, it is taking every bit of energy I have to focus on this conversation. This morning, I made a pot of coffee and proceeded to pour some of it onto my Corn Flakes. With all due respect, if you need help then you couldn't have chosen a worse person to approach."

As I finished speaking, something unsettling occurred to me. I stood up, reached out my hand, and touched Nick on the shoulder.

"Trevor, what are you doing?"

I retracted my hand and sat back down.

"Checking to see if you're real. You are. Which means you might be as crazy as me."

He grinned and said, "I'm not asking you to do any heavy lifting. Simply poke around and see what you can find. You'll get paid for your time, no matter what."

I leaned back and my chair creaked. "Why?"

"Why what?"

"Why are you doing this? I'm sure your company has the resources to track down this person. I'm a freaking train wreck, which I'm sure you noticed the second I opened up the front door. Right then and there, you could have shifted gears and told me you had come by to see how I was doing. But, here you are still pushing forward with this disastrous idea. Why?"

He shifted uncomfortably in his seat. I didn't take this cue lightly, as he didn't seem the type to let anything make him uncomfortable. After a few moments had passed, he said, "You're owed."

"Owed what?" I asked.

"I'm not sure. I don't know what you're owed or even who owes you, but Jackie talked about you a lot. She told me about what you went through when you worked narcotics and the toll it took on your life. I don't know your financial situation and maybe you already have a job, but I figured it might not be bad to offer you a chance to do something worthwhile and make some money at the same time. Jackie loved you and you ended up doing right by her. As far as I'm concerned, the house owes you some chips."

We watched each other for several moments before I spoke. "Can I think about it?"

"Sure," Nick said. "You have until the end of the week to let me know. Although the election isn't until late next year, the event schedule really gets going at the end of the month and I'd like to have some resolution before Hackney starts working rope lines and kissing babies."

I nodded and started to stand, expecting him to do the same. But he just sat there.

"Is there something else?" I asked.

Nick reached back to his coat that was draped over the back of the chair and pulled out a small bundle of papers.

I asked, "What's that?"

He held the sheets of paper in one hand and gently tapped them against the palm of the other.

"This is why I'm concerned," he said. "I don't know if you're going to take the job, but this might influence your decision. We received this through the mail. The return address simply read, 'Chaerea.'"

Nick reached out with the stack and I took the bundle. They weren't papers at all, but black and white photographs. I didn't know anything about photography, but they seemed to be high quality images. I shuffled through the pictures and each seemed to be candid shots from a variety of locations. At first glance, the one thing in common in each of the photos was the presence of presidential-hopeful Dennis Hackney. I thumbed through the photos two more times and then looked up at Nick.

"I don't get it," I admitted.

Nick smiled. "You expected to see Hackney sandwiched between two long-legged hookers?"

I shrugged. "Something like that."

"I thought the same thing. But, it appears the point of these photos is to let us know Hackney is exposed. Some of those shots were taken in private locations where media was off-limits. None of the security detail remembers seeing anyone taking photos in some of those locations."

"Any chance they were Photoshopped? Maybe they were faked just to freak you guys out."

Nick shook his head. "We verified the photos and Chaerea claims to have the negatives. The packet consists of twenty-four frames and none of them would be considered any kind of blackmail material."

"Even though the Secret Service isn't involved yet, I'm sure you could talk to Pittsburgh PD. I can put you in touch with people there."

Nick stood, retrieved his jacket, and slid it over his massive shoulders.

"We aren't there yet. We don't want to give Chaerea any publicity. Doing so may only convince him to transform what-ever fantasy he has into reality."

I wasn't sure who the "we" referred to, but I assumed it could include Hackney.

"Just think about it. Okay?"

I said I would and tried to hand him the packet of photos.

"Keep them. Those are copies. Obviously I don't have the negatives, but I was able to use the originals to make a set of duplicates for you. The images aren't as crisp as the originals, but you can see most of the details."

"Negatives?" I said. "This person didn't use a digital camera?"

Nick shook his head. "I know. It's odd. Perhaps we're looking for a photography geek. Maybe that's a place to start."

He handed me a business card, we shook hands, and he left. I stood in my living room for the longest time and thought about his offer. Although maintaining the status quo and having my body and my bank account wither away wasn't particularly appealing, I doubted I was up to any task more complicated than brushing my teeth. On the other hand, maybe the house did owe me some chips. I could get back in the game—just a little. I wasn't going to drown by dipping my toes in the water. I could put some of those well-earned chips on the table, place some safe bets, and get a feel for the game. What could it hurt?

FRAME 1

A cigarette dangling between his fingers, Dennis Hackney was leaning on a railing near an entrance ramp. A propped-open glass door is behind him and the angle of the photo indicates it was taken at ground level. A thin stream of smoke is drifting up from what he has called his only vice. The sixty-five-year-old man has spoken openly about his addiction to nicotine and has hinted he harbors animosity against those who profited by getting generations hooked on the poison. However, fearing repercussions from donors in the tobacco industry, he measures his words carefully when the topic is broached. Hackney was wearing a suit, but the tie had been loosened. He looked tired, but a polished kind of tired. Like a man who has worn fatigue all his life and knows how to wear it well.

According to Metal Security, the photo was taken after an event at the Sheraton in an area of Pittsburgh known as Station Square. The file doesn't describe the nature of the event, but with a man of Hackney's status, it could involve anything from a charity benefit to a meeting with his fellow titans of the financial industry. I don't have any reason to believe he was staying overnight at the hotel, as he has a mansion in Pittsburgh's North Hills.

Hackney's gaze seemed to be aimed to something in the distance. Something on or across the Monongahela River, I assume. The Mon flows between Station Square and downtown Pittsburgh. The file indicated the picture was taken during

14

"cocktails," but Hackney doesn't drink. His wind-down activity was right there in his hand, its smoke made a perfectly vertical path to the heavens.

I had yet to activate my now-ancient model cell phone and had no landline, so two days after Nick and I had spoken, I walked to the convenience store at the end of the block, picked up the real-life functional pay phone on the side of the building, and called Nick to accept the job. We agreed on a fee that was probably fair and he sent me the case file via email. It seemed strange Nick had sent the information from what appeared to be a personal Gmail account rather than an official Metal Security one. His business card had listed an email address of NVM@MetalSec.com but maybe he used NickVM083@gmail.com for work functions as well.

Electronic copies of the photos weren't included, so the hard copies he'd given me would have to suffice. I'd love to say I started clicking on attachments enthusiastically and devoured page after page of information that would be critical to the case. However, the attachments Nick had sent my way seemed overwhelming to me and I struggled to comprehend the data. I closed out the email and opened up a window on the screen to compose a message of my own. On two separate occasions during the day I drafted poorly written replies to Nick in which I apologized and explained I had changed my mind about helping with the case. Each time I ended up deleting the message, but I still did nothing regarding the investigation other than go through the photos Nick had given me and jot down notes in a notepad. Other than my notetaking, I did nothing. Not on day on, day two, or on day three. On day four, I traded in my sweatpants for an old pair of blue jeans that were now a little large on me.

Progress.

As if trying to push Hell away, I managed eighteen pushups. Not that many months before—yet a lifetime ago—I could easily

15

crank out fifty before running three or four miles at a decent pace. Now I was winded. The moderate dizziness I felt when I got back to my feet subsided after a few seconds. I took this to be a good sign and decided my fifth day of semi-employment would actually involve trying to do the job I was hired to perform.

I delayed taking my morning dose of pills and downed strong coffee so I could make an attempt at reading Nick's case file with a clear-ish head. The desk chair squeaked as I rolled it back. I took a seat, and scooted myself up to the desk in my living room. I moved the gray mouse with my fingertips and the monitor buzzed to life. I opened the email from Nick and saw a list of IP addresses and locations, each associated with a number. The attachments to the email were all numbered and appeared as a separate list in a box at the top of the message. I clicked on the first attachment and it opened. It was a message from Chaerea to the email address attached to Dennis Hackney's campaign website. I labored through each word and my brain tried to assemble the words into coherent strings that held meaning. At first, the words were a jumble, nothing but a chaotic pile of shards left over from a broken stained glass window. I inhaled deeply and did my best to focus my mind. The shards started to form recognizable patterns and a coherent scene began to appear in front of me.

From: Chaerea41@mailspot.com
Date: January 2
To: Hackney4POTUS@campaign.org
Subject: I know who you are
Message:
I know you. I know you better than you know yourself. You see, the only version you have ever known is the one that exists now. Today. But you have been in and out of this world many times and in numerous forms. History has witnessed your conquests. Your expeditions. Your crusades. I see the road ahead and I see it so clearly. My view is clear because I've

walked similar roads. Roads that have run parallel to yours. Roads you eventually became comfortable with seeing on the edge of your vision because to you they were just another part of the landscape. Each time this has occurred, your attention has drifted and you carried on down your path until my road intersected with yours. Suddenly. Violently.

There will be a distinction to our journey this time. With the benefit of hindsight, I will document our travels with images I will eventually disseminate to the world. Oh, yes. I will leave breadcrumbs for our future selves so hindsight can be made clearer still.

For you, this will seem like it's the first time we have come to know each other. But you are mine. Each and every time, you are mine. It's time for our tale to be told and for my narration to begin.

—Chaerea

I leaned back in my chair and read the email three more times. As well as I could manage with my fuzzy cognitive skills, I dissected the structure, wording, and tone. Part of me had been hoping Nick had simply been throwing me a softball and that I'd read the email and discover Chaerea was doing nothing more than rambling about aliens or how the government was sending radio waves into our brains and how we are all being hypnotized into complacency. Nick would check in with me in a couple of weeks and I would have tracked down Chaerea to a homeless shelter where, after being confronted, he would admit to having sent the emails from an internet café—if those even still exist. None of it would be taken too seriously. While a threat with a disorganized thought process is still a threat, it's not nearly to the same level of dangerousness as one who can organize thoughts, conduct pre-attack surveillance, acquire the necessary resources, and carry out a strategic attack. That's not what I was looking at here.

The email in front of me was no softball, it was a grenade.

While certainly being composed by someone with a seat on the crazy train, it was well-written, thoughtful, purposeful, organized, and direct. If the email was any indication, Chaerea was a legitimate threat.

I minimized Chaerea's message and glanced at the IP address list in Nick's email. The email had been sent from the Main Branch of the Carnegie Library of Pittsburgh. I knew that library. It was huge and had a fantastic collection of books. I knew that particular branch also had something else important. Cameras. They had cameras.

Deep inside, I felt a twinge. I wasn't sure, but I thought it might have been some whisper of something similar to what I used to feel when discovering I had a possible lead to follow. But the twinge was replaced with nausea when I envisioned my leaving the house and going to the library in an effort to convince staff members and security personnel to give me access to video recordings. It would be much easier if I was still a cop, which I was not and never would be again. However, I knew a cop. A big, persuasive cop who—for whatever reason—happened to like me. As a bonus, Chase wasn't opposed to doing a few things off the books. I still wasn't sure why Nick didn't want Pittsburgh PD involved officially, but I'd respect his wishes.

Realizing I needed to call Chase, I stood to go to the phone. Then I remembered I had never reactivated my home phone number. I would have called him from my cell phone, but I still hadn't activated it either. For all of Chase's qualities, he was notoriously bad about checking email. I sighed and looked at the front door I would have to pass through if I wanted to have contact with the outside world. For the first time in days, I spoke.

"Damn."

FRAME 2

The David L. Lawrence Convention Center is recognizable from a distance because of its long roof resembling a set of ski jumps. However, locals will be quick to recognize the artificial waterfalls and water-covered steps on exhibit under a portion of building. The roadway next to the waterfalls is where Dennis Hackney was entering a limousine, a member of his security team holding the door open, undoubtedly ready to pounce at the first sign of trouble. Even the lack of color in the photograph cannot hide the expensiveness of Hackney's suit and the crispness in his shirt. In spite of being captured in stride, his posture and mannerisms are magazine-model perfect.

He's leaving a manufacturing convention where he gave a thirty-minute speech before glad-handing with the region's economic elite. His eyes are cheerful, but that could be staged for any onlookers. The limo is facing the camera, and I know from the background and the positioning, the photo was taken from near the riverfront. There are a couple of blurry forms in the distance behind the limo, too far away to be recognizable. The only other person I can clearly make out in the photo is the security man holding the car door. There is a glare on the windshield and I can't see any part of the driver other than his hands and wrists.

Per Metal Security, the photo was taken a week after Hackney announced his intention to run for president. The manufacturing convention was likely a prime opportunity to solicit donations while simultaneously proclaiming to be on the side of US companies and workers. Chaerea wouldn't have had any problem getting in a position to take the photo. The streets would be open and tourists with cameras are nothing new to Pittsburgh. It was an easy shot. A really easy shot.

"The library?" Chase asked as I stood in front of his desk. The burglary squad was located on the second floor of the department's headquarters on Western Avenue.

"Right," I answered while shifting back and forth on my feet uncomfortably. "The main branch."

I could feel the eyes on me and the glares I received weren't of the happy reunion sort. While the last part of my career with the department hadn't been celebrated, my departure was.

"You want me to go with you to the library?"

I felt sweat starting to form under my blue Under Armour sweatshirt. Thanks to my institutionally aided weight loss, I was able to slink out of my black leather jacket without any effort.

I draped the jacket over one arm and said, "Yes, the library. You are familiar with the concept of libraries, right?"

"Intimately," Chase scowled and crossed his tree trunk arms. Although it was freezing outside, he was wearing a short-sleeved polo shirt that made all of his arm tattoos visible. Of course at this point, a tattoo artist would have difficulty finding a section of blank canvas on his body. "And while I respect your love of the written word," he continued, "I am curious as to why you want me to join you."

"I have some questions to ask their staff," I said.

"Questions."

I nodded.

"Questions like, 'Hey, do you have a copy of *Six Days of the Condor* available?'"

"Possibly."

Chase's jaw tightened and his tone became foreboding.

"Trevor."

"Chase."

"Trevor. No."

He was raising his voice and whoever had not been looking our way certainly was now.

"Chase. Yes."

He unfolded the tree trunks and leaned over his desk. "Tell me you're not working a case."

"I'm not working a case."

He leaned back slightly and started to relax. Then his skepticism kicked in.

"Is that true?"

"No."

"Goddamn it, Trevor!"

He leapt up, causing his chair to roll backwards and slam into the front of another detective's, desk. All activity in the cubicle farm came to a halt. I couldn't remember if Chase was six feet four inches tall or six foot five. But at that moment, he appeared to be a full ten feet of rage.

Chase realized we'd become the center of attention, turned his head side to side, and projected menacing glares at each of his colleagues. The room erupted with sounds as conversations resumed and keyboards were pecked. He leaned forward, placed his hands on the desk, and directed his stare at me.

He opened his mouth to speak, but I interrupted. "I know what you're going to say. You're going to say you think I'm not ready to start working cases again. You're going to say I'm rushing things and being reckless. You're going to tell me that I need to find a job I can perform in a detached manner so I don't become obsessed or overly stressed."

I paused. Chase didn't speak, but his expression did.

"Look. It's kind of an interesting case and it has nothing to do with drugs or murder. You see, that guy Dennis Hackney who is running for—"

Chase lifted one of his hands and held up a single finger. To my surprise, it was his index finger. He reached into a desk drawer, removed a folder, laid it on the desk, and spun it around so the pages were facing my direction. Without saying a word, he opened the folder so I could see the contents. This wasn't an official folder, it was his personal folder. He started flipping through the pages one by one. He didn't give me time to read the details of the reports, but it wasn't necessary. The photos attached to the reports told the story.

The first pages included reports written on the day I was rescued from a sadistic drug gang that had held me captive and turned me into an addict. Seeing the photos of the chair to which I'd been strapped and the detailed images of my countless wounds and track marks hit me like a truck. The next few pages covered a cold case I'd been asked to investigate long after I'd been asked to leave the police department and not that long after I'd been forced to give up my job as an investigator with the district attorney's office. The images paper clipped to the reports included not only the initial crime scene photos that were taken before I'd become involved with the case, but also images of a few more bodies—and parts of bodies—that had been taken after my arrival. There was also a mugshot of a man who had tracked me to a rural town and tried to kill me. Not my best memory. The next few pages covered my involvement in a case brought to me by a client who had asked to meet with me about her brother's unsolved murder. She concluded our meeting by putting a bullet in her brain. The final pages covered the reason I'd been incarcerated and medicated for the past few years. There were photos taken from a bar—a hallway covered in blood, some of it mine. More photos from a store that repaired and sold record players and turntables. More death.

Chase hesitated, seemed to engage in some internal debate, and then flipped to the final item in the folder. It was a picture of Special Agent Jackie Fontree of the United States Secret Service. To me, she was simply Jackie. Her eyes were open. Her eyes were lifeless. I turned away and swallowed hard.

"Not this road," said Chase. "Not this time."

My eyes watered and I struggled to inhale. The pain and feelings of guilt I'd been trying to bury with medication and therapy sessions came rushing back.

My voice was failing, but I managed to whisper, "That's not fair."

The anger drained from Chase's face. "No. But, it's real."

Chase retrieved his chair and we sat across from each other for half a minute before I said, "I don't know what else to do. I'm afraid of what will happen if I work cases, but I think I'm more afraid of what will happen if I don't."

Chase closed the folder on the desk.

He said, "Trevor, I don't know what will happen if you stop working cases. However, I know I can help you work thorough those issues."

I nodded.

"But I can guarantee what will happen if you do start working cases again," he said. "If I even suspect you are conducting an investigation, I'm going to arrest you for performing duties as an unlicensed private investigator and anything else I can dream up. I'll do whatever is necessary to lock you away—whether it be prison or a psychiatric unit. I'll put you away, Trevor. Because I love you, man."

I stood to leave and slid into my jacket.

"And Trevor."

"Yeah."

"When you walked in here, you passed by two desks before getting to mine. What were the last names on the name plates sitting on top of those desks?"

An odd question, but I thought for a second.

"Maurer and Kelly. Why?"

Chase's shoulders fell and concern radiated from his body.

"Take your fucking meds, or I'll personally throw you in a rubber room. That's a promise."

* * *

I didn't go to the library. I didn't follow up on any IP addresses. I didn't conduct any interviews or watch any footage recorded from security cameras. After my conversation with Chase, I sat in my car and gazed out the windshield as snow began to fall on the city although I didn't really see the flakes, but only the images leftover from what Chase had shown me. Jackie. I saw Jackie—alive in my memories, gone in this life. In a heartbeat, our relationship had rekindled and was extinguished just as quickly. Avenging her murder hadn't balanced the scales, it only added weight to my own side and time wasn't significantly healing any of the wounds I had endured. Chase was right and I had delayed in taking my meds, which was why I was starting to develop a sense of purpose and an ability to focus. I'd rectify that as soon as I got back to my house. And to hell with the case. Nick Van Metre may have had the best of intentions, but I wasn't going to have anything to do with him, Metal Security, or Dennis Hackney. I was going to get my head as straight as possible and get some mindless job where nobody died if—when—I screwed up.

My own case folder, including the photographs of Hackney, were in the passenger seat. I snatched them up, got out of my car, and scanned the parking lot. At the far end of the lot sat a dumpster, hinges on the lid rusted to oblivion. I walked over and with one hand lifted the lid enough that I was able to slip the folder through with my other. Nick said he had made a set of copies, so my set wouldn't be missed.

A spell of dizziness hit me and I used the corner of the dumpster to steady myself. Another mental snapshot of Jackie's corpse flashed through my head and I vomited what little I'd eaten. After a minute, I returned to my car and told myself that I'd call Nick as soon as I'd gotten control of my emotions. He'd have to understand I couldn't be involved with any type of investigation. Of course, I never got to tell him. Nick was already dead.

FRAME 3

To call the Duquesne Club on Sixth Avenue exclusive is an understatement. Founded in 1873, the membership has included the elite of Pittsburgh society, embracing only those reaching the absolute highest levels of success in the fields of business and politics. As Dennis Hackney fit the bill in both of those categories, he was a regular at the club. The building is filled with extravagance and it would be hard to put a price tag on the fine pieces of art and carefully-chosen furnishings. Therefore, access to the building is restricted and security and discretion are priorities. So when Chaerea managed to take a photograph of Dennis Hackney having a private conversation in an otherwise empty hallway, it raised the stakes for Metal Security. The face of the other party to the conversation was turned mostly away from the camera and his identity was not known to the security firm. The other man's hands were in focus and a dark ring was visible around one finger.

Nick Van Metre had noted that Hackney stated he did not know the identity of the man, who appeared to be a good three or four inches shorter than the businessman-turned-politician. According to the notes, Hackney was there having dinner with friends and excused himself from the table to use the restroom. Hackney used the facilities down the hallway and while on his way back to the dining room, the man approached him and wished him well on his political endeavors. The two parted company and Hackney returned to his dinner table. Subsequent interviews were conducted with Duquesne Club staff, and nobody could remember the identity of the man, nor did any of the employees or regular guests remember seeing anyone taking photographs. Metal Security gained access to the club's security footage and nothing unusual was detected, and there were no other indications that an unauthorized individual had entered the building.

"Are there any firearms in the house?"

"No," I answered truthfully.

"You'd be the first former cop I've talked to who doesn't own at least one gun."

"I might be the first former cop you've talked to who has been adjudicated mentally incompetent and is prohibited from owning a firearm."

The detective, a woman named Elisa Hayes, gestured to my kitchen table. The two of us sat down and I brushed some crumbs off the table and onto the floor. I couldn't remember when I'd last eaten anything at the table, so I had no idea how long the crumbs had been there.

Her partner, who had introduced himself as Lincoln Bayless, was on the young side and had fallen into what seemed to be the latest fashion trend for that generation, which meant he was gelling his hair toward the sky while keeping a neatly-trimmed beard pointed toward the ground. Both were dressed better than your average Pittsburgh detectives and were in great contrast to me since I'd returned to sweatpants mode in the three days since Chase had set me straight.

"Would that be okay?" asked Hayes.

I was on my meds again. Every dose. On time.

"I'm sorry. What were you saying?"

"We'd like to take a look around your house?"

I glanced at Bayless who was standing in the corner with his arms crossed. For a cop, crossing one's arms is terrible from a tactical standpoint. However, he must have taken one look at me in my current state and perceived I didn't present much of a physical threat. In fact, I wasn't much of a mental threat either since I had totally forgotten why these two were in my house.

"Why are you here?" I asked for what was probably the second or third time.

The investigators exchanged a look but, to their credit, they remained patient and professional.

"We are investigating the murder of Nick Van Metre," said Hayes.

I rubbed my face and felt the abrasive, unkempt whiskers. Involuntarily, I glanced at Bayless's photo-shoot-ready beard.

"Mr. Galloway?"

"I'm sorry, Detective..."

"Hayes," she reminded me.

"I'm sorry, Detective Hayes. My medication prevents me from concentrating and seems to affect my short-term memory. Did you say Nick Van Metre is dead?"

Bayless stepped forward and I reflexively shrunk back. It was a total overreaction on my part. He stopped, unfolded his arms, and held his hands up in a conciliatory manner.

"Whoa there, buddy. Nobody wants to hurt you."

"Okay," I said meekly.

Bayless said, "As we told you when we arrived, Nick Van Metre was fished out of the Allegheny River yesterday. It looks like he'd been in there for at least three days and we are retracing his movements in the days before he died. He worked for a company called—"

"Metal Security!" I said with a sense of self-satisfaction before realizing the inappropriateness of my being happy about remembering something.

"Right," he said. "The vice president of the company told us Mr. Van Metre had been in contact with you and wanted to enlist your help with an investigation. It had something to do with Dennis Hackney."

I nodded.

"Mr. McGillicuddy stated that you may have received some photographs of Dennis Hackney and that Mr. Van Metre wanted you to obtain the identity of a potential stalker."

"Who?" I asked.

"Ric McGillicuddy is the VP of Metal Security that we mentioned. He was Nick's right hand man."

"Okay," I said.

There was an awkward pause in the conversation that was broken when I said, "Did you say you wanted to search my house for something?"

Hayes leaned back and crossed her legs, which would have been another tactical mistake had I been able to pose any kind of danger. Her foot dangled under the edge of the table, just below my line of sight.

She said, "We'd like to check for weapons, for our safety."

The statement puzzled me, but most things did as of late.

I shook my head. "I don't have any weapons."

Had I said that a few minutes ago? Had they asked me that question already?

"We understand," said Bayless. "But you can never be too careful. Right?"

"Right," I said.

Then I thought, *they might was well start right here in the kitchen.* I was turning my head from side to side, then I froze. They were interviewing me—a known nutcase—in the kitchen.

Hayes shifted in her chair and readjusted her legs. "Is something wrong, Mr. Galloway?"

I didn't breathe. I didn't blink. My mind was trying to process facts I'd once been able to recall automatically, but now struggled to grasp.

Finally, I said, "I don't know anything about Nick's murder."

Bayless moved a half step closer. "We didn't say you did, sir."

"What are you looking for?" I asked.

Hayes uncrossed her legs and I caught sight of her foot before she placed it on the floor. "We're concerned about weap—"

"What are you really looking for?" I said.

Bayless moved in another step. "Now stay calm, Mr. Galloway. This is just routine. We would like to make sure the area is safe and then talk about what Mr. Van Metre had you looking into. Perhaps if you gave us a look at the photographs you were given, then we could better understand what Mr. Van Metre was into."

"What he was into? Why don't you review the Metal Security files? They have the original photos."

At the mention of originals, the detectives exchanged a look.

Bayless said, "It appears Mr. Van Metre wasn't sharing everything with the company. In fact, he may have been involved in some improprieties."

"I see," I said. Silence filled the kitchen until an alarm beeped on my wristwatch. I pressed a button to silence the noise. "Well, I threw those photos in the trash days ago. As you can see, I'm in no condition to be helping anyone with any kind of investigation."

I tapped my watch. "My meds," I explained. "I have to take my medication right now. It's mandated by the courts. You understand."

Bayless moved back a step. I stood and moved to a cabinet. I opened the cabinet door, reached up, retrieved a pill bottle from one shelf and pulled down a glass form another. I set both of the items on the counter. I never cared much about the appearance of my kitchen, so I've never had it remodeled. In fact, the cabinets are original to the house, which was built sometime in the eighties. I've had to replace a couple of the hinges, but I never got around to replacing the ones on the door that was open in front of me.

I made a show of trying to open my pill bottle. After a failed third attempt, Bayless sighed and walked in my direction to help me out.

"Here, let me help," he said while moving my way.

"Thank you," I said.

Before he could completely close the distance, I tossed the pill bottle in his direction so he would have to reach up to make the catch. As fast as I could, I grabbed the open cabinet door and ripped it off its hinges. I took two quick strides across the kitchen, leveled the door so it was parallel to the floor, and swung the door into Bayless's right knee. Multiple things cracked and I'm not sure which sound was the splintering of wood and which was the shattering of the kneecap, but a lot of screaming followed. I then dropped the cabinet door, rushed toward the kitchen table, and pushed it into Hayes, who was starting to stand and draw a gun from a holster on her right hip. The impact of the table on her thighs knocked her over, but she managed to get the weapon out of her holster. A shot went past my head and into my refrigerator. I hurdled Bayless who was rolling around on the floor trying to pull his own gun. After stumbling against a wall, I managed to pinball off the hard surface and regain my balance before racing through the living room and out my front door.

My sprint, if you could call it that after the first fifty yards, ended when I reached the convenience store at the corner. I dialed 9-1-1 from the payphone and got the units rolling this way. Then I debated calling Chase. We hadn't spoken since he made it clear what he'd do if he found me sniffing around a case. I had taken his advice, but I wondered if he would believe me. An elderly woman walked by and eyed me suspiciously. I was sweating, breathing heavily, and horribly underdressed for the weather, but she was kind enough to give me change to make the call. Of course Chase would believe me. He was my best friend.

"This is hard to believe," Chase said as crime scene units combed through my house.

We were standing in the front yard and I had yet to be permitted to return inside. Several of my neighbors were gawking from their own yards and peering through windows at the activity. Most of them had witnessed a similar scene on a night twenty-five months prior when I had been taken into custody and placed into the back of a police vehicle. Given the graphic media accounts detailing my breakdown and the ensuing bloodbath, I'm sure fear of retaliation was the only reason there hadn't been an organized neighborhood protest regarding my return.

I stared at Chase who wasn't impressed by my story regarding Nick Van Metre hiring me to assist him, the threats to Dennis Hackney, and the two fake cops who had entered my home. My mind was fuzzy, but I thought I had conveyed the sequence of events correctly.

"I'm sorry, man. You're telling me Nick Van Metre, a guy who should hate you, agreed to hire a former mental patient who went on a killing spree to investigate threats made toward a man running for president of the United States."

"Right."

"And now two police impersonators entered your house, for purposes unknown, and you managed to fight them off with kitchen cabinetry so you could escape."

I shook my head. "I only used the cabinetry on one of them. I knocked the other one over with a table before she took a shot at me."

"So we should be able to dig a bullet out of a wall."

"I think it hit my refrigerator," I said. "The bullet whizzed past my head, so it might be somewhere in my icebox."

Chase asked, "Did the shooter yell *freeze* first?"

I stared at my friend.

"I don't feel like this conversation is going well," I observed.

"The neighbors didn't hear anything. Nobody called nine-one-one," he said.

"My neighbors are old," I reminded him. "They're probably watching *Matlock* reruns with the volume on full blast."

Chase rolled his neck around the way he does when he's exercising as much patience as he capable of doing. "Well, I did confirm that the department didn't have any detectives here. What made you think these two weren't real cops?"

"A few things," I said. "They claimed to be concerned I might have a weapon in the house and be some sort of threat. However, the man, Bayless, crossed his arms and the woman, Hayes, crossed her legs. Both of them repeatedly put themselves in positions of disadvantage and they interviewed me in the kitchen."

Chase nodded. Any cop knows not to interview a subject in the kitchen. There are way too many sharp objects within arm's reach.

"Also, they were dressed a little too nice."

"Anything else?" he asked.

"Heels. I didn't notice at first, but Hayes was wearing heels. Not high-heels, but still. Other than on television, what female cop wears heals when on duty?"

Chase nodded, unconvinced I wasn't describing actions taken by figments of my imagination.

"Did they show you badges?"

I didn't answer.

"Trevor, did they show you any badges?"

"I don't know," I muttered. "I don't remember inviting them in. It's cloudy."

"You don't know? You're a former narcotics detective who has been hunted by a drug gang and you don't know if two strangers claiming to be law enforcement officers properly identified themselves?" Chase asked incredulously.

I shivered from the cold. Nobody had offered me a coat.

"I can't remember," I said.

"You can't remember? Are you kidding me?"

"Hey, look," I shot back. "You didn't want to hear about the case and you told me to take my fucking meds! So, that means I'm living in a fog and you're going to have to suffer through me not being clear on a few things. But I'm telling you, people came into my house and I think they wanted to find out

32

how much I knew and if I still had the photos Nick gave me."

"The photos someone took of Dennis Hackney?"

"Right."

"Do you have them? Can I see them?"

I hesitated. "What day is it?"

Chase sighed. "Wednesday."

"On what day do they empty the dumpster outside your office?"

Chase gave me a puzzled look. "I'm not sure. Mondays, I think."

"Then, no. I don't have the photos."

Chase cocked his head and pursed his lips.

"But, I have emails from Nick. You'll be able to see those."

A crime scene tech walked out the front door of the house and made a beeline for Chase.

"And your crime scene guys are about to give you forensic evidence that will back my story."

Chase pulled his coat around his body, rubbed his face, and turned toward the man. "Watcha got, Tom?"

The man spat on the ground and shrugged. "A broken cabinet and an overturned table."

"And?" I asked.

The tech shot me a sideways glance. "And what?"

"And the hole in my refrigerator? Maybe a shell casing on the floor?"

The man looked at me as if I had three heads and then addressed Chase. "There's no refrigerator in there, but there was one at some point. We certainly didn't find any shell casings. Also, we didn't find any fingerprints on the table. Not even Mr. Galloway's."

Chase shot me a glance. "Dude. Where's your refrigerator. I *know* you had a refrigerator."

I wasn't sure what to say. My heart sank. How long did it take me to run to the store and call the police? How long was the response time? The total time elapsed couldn't have been more than ten minutes. The bastards somehow removed my refrigerator and hauled it away in a matter of minutes? That seemed impossible. It seemed...insane.

FRAME 4

Sixty miles north of Pittsburgh, there is an old limestone mine. Although no longer home to an active mining operation, Iron Mountain still serves a purpose. The underground facility is home to multiple companies and federal entities that have requirements for security, storage capacity, and environmental controls. In the heart of working-class Pennsylvania, the employees who filter through the ant farm caverns represent a key demographic important to those with political ambitions.

Dennis Hackney sat smiling in the passenger seat of a golf cart that was set to travel down some of the twenty miles of paved roads twisting throughout the mountain. Forgoing his usual business suit, Hackney decided to dress in slacks and a button-down shirt with no tie. His sleeves were rolled up on his forearms, the folds making perfect triangles. No doubt the wardrobe decision was intentional and meant to convey that the multi-millionaire was just a regular Joe, like all those hard-working people slogging their way into the windowless cave on a daily basis. His usual gold Rolex was missing, but the broad wedding band with embedded diamonds wasn't and it seemed a bit flashy for this crowd. A glimmer of light caught on it in the photo, making it stand out. When the shot was taken, the driver of the golf cart, the CEO of the facility, had his mouth open as if he was in midsentence. He must have said something to amuse the visiting candidate, therefore generating the laugh.

To access the mine, employees and visitors had to enter a

security checkpoint, scan an access card, and pass through a magnetometer. Four Metal Security employees are visible in the background and it's impossible to tell if they are armed in the photo. None of the four were Nick. I can't imagine more than four operatives would accompany Hackney into a secure facility, so he must have sat this one out. Perhaps he stayed with the spouse since she doesn't appear to be present at this event.

The photo was taken from head-on and there was no indication the photographer was sneaking a shot from a position of concealment. This was bold. This was direct. This was unflinching infiltration.

"I've been taking my medication, so don't try to convince me I'm hallucinating."

Chase didn't speak and kept walking to the desk where my computer sat. I moved the mouse and the monitor came to life. I accessed my email account and scanned the listing of my messages. My breath caught.

"Can you pull up any of the emails from Nick Van Metre?" Chase asked.

The messages should have been on top. With my social skills and history, it's not like I had a lot of friends checking on me. Other than a Nigerian prince letting me know about a fantastic investment opportunity and a pharmaceutical company concerned about my penis size, I don't think I'd received any other emails since I'd been released into the world.

"Hold on," I said, trying not to sound panicked.

I filtered the emails by the sender name. No hits for *Van Metre*. No hits for *NickVM083*. No hits when I searched for the terms *Metal Security*, *Chaerea*, *Hackney*, or *photos*.

"They're gone," I said.

Chase walked over to my living room couch and plopped down.

I turned from the computer and faced him. "Chase, I'm not

hallucinating. I've been taking my medication."

He stared straight ahead. He couldn't make eye contact with me.

"Chase, there were two—"

"Stop," he interrupted. "Just stop."

We didn't say anything for nearly a minute while I tried to mentally comb through the events of the day. Doubts started to creep in on me from the periphery. Trust is a hard thing to earn once it's lost, and I had betrayed myself several times in the past.

"Do you remember when I walked in this room and took you into custody?"

"Yes."

"You were sitting right here on the couch."

I remembered.

"Later, you told me you hadn't been sitting here alone. They were real in your mind, weren't they?"

"I suppose," I admitted.

"Now you're talking about phantom police impersonators, nonexistent emails, and an important case that a security firm couldn't handle so they brought in the legendary and infamous Trevor 'Tin Man' Galloway."

I opened my mouth to speak, but the words wouldn't come.

"I have to call homicide," Chase said. "They are going to have to talk to you."

"Homicide?" I asked. "So, you do believe that someone tried to kill me?"

Chase shook his head. "I'm calling homicide because it's true that a man named Nick Van Metre was murdered. In fact, he was pulled out of the Allegheny and it looks like someone worked him over pretty good before he drowned. They found restraint marks on his wrists and ankles, like he'd been bound to a chair." Chase scanned the street as was his habit. "Apparently, Nick had dialed nine-one-one a day prior and said he thought someone had broken into his house. But before units could respond, he called back to say it was a false alarm. Anyway, you're going to have to talk to some people."

"So, you want me to fill in the homicide guys on my interactions with Nick?"

Chase didn't answer. He looked away. Then I got it.

"Oh," I said. "You think they might consider me a person of interest."

"Trevor, I—"

I held up a hand. "It's okay. I get it. *Unstable, Delusional Maniac Claims to Have Been Recruited by Recently Deceased Murder Victim* is quite the headline. You have to get in front of something like that."

"It's not necessarily going to be a headline," he said. "But, it would be negligent of them to not interview you. If you really have had contact with Van Metre, then they need to know."

If.

My only friend in the world said *If.*

Now my brain was whispering *If.*

But I had spoken to him. I had reached out and touched Nick.

If.

The homicide detectives didn't like me. Although they didn't know me personally, they knew my reputation. Prior to being rescued from the drug gang that had abducted me, I'd been doped up and tortured to the point I'd given up the names of informants, undercover officers, and other crucial operational details. It's not that cops are immune to understanding, but understanding has its limits. When trust is broken into a million shards, even when the seeds of empathy have been planted, forgiveness dies on the vine.

For ninety minutes, the detectives had me go over my conversations with Nick. My living room became their interrogation room, because I'd refused to let them whisk me away so I could sit on an uncomfortable metal chair in a tiny room wired for audio and video. No way. I wasn't under arrest and was in fact the victim, so I decided I wasn't going anywhere.

The pivotal part of the conversation came when they asked

me for my alibis for the possible break-in at Nick's house and then for the estimated time of death. The best I could figure, I had been home either watching television or sleeping at either of those times, so that was no help. They asked for proof that I'd been paid by Metal Security. I hadn't been paid yet, so that was no help. They asked if I'd been taking all of my medication as prescribed. Chase helpfully chimed in and told them I'd been late taking some of my pills, so that was no help. Finally, they asked if they could search the house and I told them they could go to hell, so that was no help.

It was getting dark by the time the guys from homicide wrapped things up. It was clear I was now a person of interest in the death of Nick Van Metre, in spite of there being no evidence against me. The good news was, there was no proof Nick and I had any contact over the past two years. The bad news was, there was no proof Nick and I had any contact over the past two years. My case for innocence was also a strong case for insanity.

Chase stood in the doorway and watched the other detectives drive away. I was standing in the middle of my living room and he didn't turn to look at me.

"I had to call them. It was unavoidable. You know that, right?" he said.

"Yes."

"You're still my friend, Trevor."

"I know."

"I don't want you to hurt anyone, including yourself."

"I know that too."

"Do you have a gun?"

"No," I said truthfully. "It was forfeited as part of my court proceedings and now I can't legally purchase one."

"There could still be some drug gang members looking to do you harm," he said.

I shrugged. "I killed most of the ones that gave a damn."

"They could still come after you. You have to be careful."

"Damnit, Chase. Do you want me to have a gun or not?"

He didn't answer.

"Look, as soon as you leave I'm going to take my pills and return to zombie mode. Once I do that, it won't matter. Five drug gangs could burst in here intending to beat me to death and I'd probably think they were delivering Indian food. I'm sure you're right and I dreamed up this whole cop impersonation business. I'll talk to my doctor and see if he can adjust my medication."

He turned toward me and asked, "Is there anything you need right now?"

"No. I'm fine. We're fine. I'm sorry I caused so much trouble."

Chase took a step outside and closed the door behind him. The quiet of the house felt heavy. My head felt the weight of the day and I decided to follow through with what I'd told Chase. I went to the kitchen and looked around for the pill bottle I'd thrown to the real or imagined Detective Bayless. No pills. The crime scene techs wouldn't have taken them, so where were they? Fine, I'd call my psychiatrist tomorrow, explain what happened, and get a refill. In the meantime I was starving, so I took a step toward my refrigerator. Damn. No refrigerator. I snooped around in the cabinets—the ones that still had doors—and the best I could come up with was a box of Honey Nut Cheerios. I reached into the box, scooped out a handful, and put it in my mouth. Stale. I swiveled my head and took in the disaster of the kitchen, complete with fingerprint dust on the table that had been placed upright, and decided I needed to get out of the house for a few minutes. Getting a quiet meal and taking the opportunity to gather my scattered thoughts might do me some good. I needed some alone time. Over the past few years, aloneness has become a reliable companion.

FRAME 5

The modernization project at Pittsburgh International Airport was expected to generate over $1.7 billion in economic activity, create thousands of jobs, and enhance the customer experience for those who traveled in and out of the airport as well as those who frequented the many shops and restaurants that were located outside the secure area. As a major investor in the project, Dennis Hackney was asked to cut the ceremonial ribbon to kick off the massive facelift. The lack of color in the photo did nothing to dull the shine of the oversized scissors being held by Hackney as he made the cut on the ribbon that carried the text HOW FAR CAN WE GO?

The surrounding VIPs are clapping, each looking in the same direction, presumably toward a pocket of photographers to their left. Whoever took this photo wasn't with the rest of the press. He or she was positioned forty-five degrees in the other direction. The picture was taken outdoors near a tarmac. There is a blurred figure deep in the background. From the posture, it's possible it's a member of the security detail.

Something is different about Hackney. The billboard grin is there, but there's nothing authentic behind the display of whitened teeth. Under his eyes are hints of dark circles and his six-foot-two frame seems smaller somehow. This photo shows a man with shoulders that are broad but carry significant weight. Hackney has a strong business pedigree, but one has to wonder what kind of toll a presidential campaign will take on a man with no foundation in politics. The pages of history are filled with stories of societies that rewarded the zealotry of its aspiring leaders. But, in the end, both the populace and the zealot pay a price that is higher than anyone could have anticipated.

Applebee's doesn't exactly require formal attire, but I shaved for the first time in days before changing into a pair of jeans and old University of Akron sweatshirt. The sweatshirt was one of my favorites and I liked representing the school that was kind enough to accept me after I'd been kicked out of the Virginia Military Institute because of my temper. While VMI, being a military college, had a certain appreciation for aggression, beating an upperclassman unconscious fell outside their acceptable parameters. Since I was by myself, I figured I'd grab a seat at the bar and eat while watching ESPN personalities dissect NFL games for which I cared nothing these days.

There wasn't much of a Wednesday night crowd, so I had my pick of stools and found one with a view of a television. Predictably, a sports reporter was interviewing the starting strong safety of one of teams remaining in the playoffs. The player looked like maybe he'd finished a workout and was wearing a tight tech gear shirt with no sleeves. He had muscles. His muscles had muscles. I thought about how I used to have a few muscles and how ripping my cabinet door off had taken much more effort than it should have. I had to get back in shape. I needed ten or fifteen pounds of healthy weight and cardiovascular abilities greater than that of a box turtle. My mind might never be right, but it was time to get my body right. It would be quite a climb, but I was going to start eating right and converting those calories into results. I was going to get strong. I was going to become agile.

The bartender, a cute redhead in her late twenties or early thirties, appeared in front of me. "Can I get you something to drink?"

Tomorrow. I would work on strong and agile tomorrow.

"A Sam Adams please."

She returned with the drink and looked down at my chest. "Akron, huh? My sister went there. Maybe you—"

She looked at my face and blushed. I'm in my mid-forties, but most people would guess I was at least fifty. Oddly, I think I appeared to be even older a few years ago but my high-mileage aging process seemed to have slowed.

"You probably didn't know her," she said with an embarrassed grin.

I didn't try to smile back, because a smile on my face rarely comes across as sincere. So, I substituted the expression for words. "Hey, I'm not that old," I said. "And I was there a long time. It took me a while to graduate. I had a problem with being late for my classes."

"Oh," said Bethany. At least her name tag read *Bethany*. "Problems making the morning classes?"

I nodded. "Yes. But to be fair, we had to tell time using sundials back then. They make for terrible alarm clocks."

Now she gave me the full smile, pointed at me, and said. "You're funny."

"I'm really not," I replied truthfully.

I took a long drink of my beer, finished that one and had an appetizer and a couple more drinks while Bethany and I talked about everything and nothing. For a little while, I forgot about Nick Van Metre. I didn't think about Jackie. I gave my mind a break from a history of violence, retribution, and addiction. I found a little island surrounded by calm waters. Was this how normal people felt most of the time? Like many things of late, I couldn't remember. But for one night—just one damn night—I didn't want to remember anything. One tiny oasis of amnesia without the risk of addiction. Was that too much to ask?

She yawned and stretched her arms above her head. The sheet fell and her small breasts lifted. A black circle was tattooed on the back of her left shoulder. Inside the circle, the artist had created the shape of a spider out of the negative space—Bethany's white skin contrasting brilliantly with the dark ink. The detail created by the use of negative space was perfect. It's incredible the detail one could see when examining what isn't there.

Her shoulder, like the rest of her body, showed muscle tone one wouldn't expect from an aspiring novelist who spends her nights tending bar at a chain restaurant. Her arms lowered and she rubbed her eyes with one hand. The bed was warm and smelled like a lavender paradise. My eyes were open, but I didn't move. After a few seconds, she turned her torso and noticed me watching her.

"Hey, you," she said with a smile.

"Hey, yourself."

"Bethany," she said.

"I remember," I said. "Bethany Nolan. You're originally from Ironton, Ohio. You have an older sister who works in Newport, Kentucky, and a younger brother who is working on a degree in finance. Your sister's name is Tina and your brother's name is Lance."

"Impressive. You have a good memory."

The compliment should have boosted my ego, but the improvement in my ability to recollect could be interpreted as foreshadowing.

"And why am I twenty-seven and tending bar?"

"To pay your way through stripper school."

She punched me playfully in the stomach.

"You were right. You're not funny."

"To save up enough money to get by while you give writing a shot. You've written two yet-to-be-published novels, but recently landed a literary agent."

"Not bad."

"Thank you."

"But it was *three* yet-to-be-published novels."

She laid back down beside me, bent one arm, and propped

her head up to better look at me.

Her abs flexed and as she settled in. She noticed me looking and glanced down at herself.

"What?" she asked.

"Do you workout, or come by that naturally?"

"I take Krav Maga classes three times a week."

I was familiar with the self-defense system that had been developed for military and security forces in Israel. It involves elements of boxing, wrestling, judo, karate, and aikido and emphasizes avoiding conflict if possible, but ending a fight with extreme aggression if necessary. I didn't know her well, but I was having difficulty imagining Bethany becoming aggressive. Of course, more than once I'd been accused of radiating a quiet sense of aggression, so perhaps I wasn't the best person to assess the volatility of others.

"And you're Trevor," she said.

"I am."

"You were a cop."

"I was."

"Now you aren't."

"Nope."

She paused to see if I had more to add. I didn't, so she continued.

"You occasionally get asked to consult on cases, but you aren't working anything now."

"You have a good memory too. Maybe you should be a detective. You could be a novelist and a detective, like in that television show."

"You like old music."

"That's not true," I said defensively.

"Last night you made references to Skid Row, Warrant, and Tesla."

"Those bands are legendary and I like you, so maybe we should change the subject before you *really* manage to offend me."

She laughed and said, "Fine. You told me you aren't married, but I didn't ask if you'd ever been."

"I haven't."

"Would it be rude to ask why?"

"Absolutely."

"Okay. Why haven't you been married?"

"Which cliché would you like? Take your pick."

She moved her other hand to her chin and produced an exaggerated expression of concentration.

"I'll go with 'I just never met the right woman.'"

"Ah. A classic. I do love the classics."

She took her hand off her chin and waved off the answer. "Wait, no. I'll go with 'I've been close a couple of times, but things just didn't work out.'"

"I do love listening to the greatest hits."

"Fine." She laughed. "I'll just make up a reason."

"Make it a good one," I said.

"Do you drink coffee?"

"That's hardly a reason to not get married."

"No," she said. "The question is unrelated to your extended bachelorhood."

"I bleed coffee."

She laid her head on the pillow, pulled the blankets over her porcelain body, and closed the lids over her bright blue eyes.

"Good. The coffee maker is in the kitchen and you'll find the coffee can and filters beside it on the counter. Make a full pot, will you?"

I got out of bed, found my clothes, and got dressed.

Before I made it to the bedroom door, she said, "Oh, and try to be quiet. My roommate is probably still asleep and she's definitely not a morning person."

I wasn't sure we were being quiet the night before, but I walked softly down the hall. The kitchen was typical of a two-bedroom apartment, so nothing was hard to find. I got the coffee started and found some mugs in a cabinet. I grabbed the mugs with one hand and clumsily clinked them together. I cringed and hoped I hadn't woken up the roommate, but a few seconds later I heard footsteps coming down the darkened hallway. I mentally prepared an apology while hoping the roommate wouldn't scream at seeing a stranger in her kitchen.

Long hair hung down from the silhouette coming down the hall, but something seemed off with the form and movements. The walk, which included a subtle lateral swaying, was somehow familiar. As the figure drew closer, the contours and mannerisms became more male than female. Then the figure emerged from the darkness and into the light and the man held his arms open as if waiting for an embrace.

"Trevor," he said, with a Lithuanian accent.

"Lukas," I replied.

"No hug for an old friend?"

I put the mugs on the table and put my hands in the pockets of my jeans. A tactical disadvantage in most cases, but only when the other party has a heartbeat.

"Hard pass," I said quietly.

He leaned against a wall and brushed greasy strands of hair away from his face.

"It has been a while, my friend."

"We aren't friends."

"Oh, come now." He unbuttoned his white shirt and held it open. "What are a few bullet holes between friends?"

Blood trickled from fresh bullet wounds, the crimson streaking down and branching through his black and gray tattoos.

I jutted my chin toward the damage and said, "You should get that looked at."

"Do you think?" He stepped forward and let his shirt fall back into place. "Let me ask you, Mr. Galloway. In your professional opinion, what is my prognosis?"

I picked up one of the mugs, turned toward the coffee maker, and poured myself a cup. When I turned back, his face was six inches from my nose.

"Still fatal," I answered before turning my head and taking a sip of coffee. I swallowed the pleasantly hot liquid and then added, "Unfortunately, I can only kill you once."

Lukas smirked and our eyes locked. "Where is this journey taking us this time, Trevor? Are we going to misbehave?"

"Not this time, Lukas."

"Who's Lukas?" Bethany asked as she walked into the kitchen. She was covered by a long T-shirt with the logo for a band called Nothing More. Without hesitation, she moved to within arm's reach of the intruder. She picked up the other coffee mug from the table and went to get her own cup of coffee.

Lukas Derela looked from her to me and flashed an ominous smile.

"He's nobody," I said. "Sometimes I talk to myself."

Bethany came near me, put her hand on my face, leaned in and whispered, "Well, when you're finished with your conversation maybe you can join me and we can work on our oral skills together."

I watched her walk down the hallway and disappear into her bedroom.

I turned toward my former captor and said, "You can stick around and watch if you want. I don't care anymore. There's nothing more you can do to me."

He laughed. "That's funny! Nothing more. Like the words on the pretty girl's shirt."

A wave of concern washed over me.

"That is quite a coincidence, is it not? She wears a shirt with words you were no doubt thinking when you saw me. How lucky that you met a beautiful, young girl who wanted to sleep with an old, broken down detective. Did she ask about your past? Did she press you for details?"

He made a tsk-tsk sound with his tongue. His eyes morphed into something reptilian. "How fortunate she asked questions that required the vaguest of responses."

"Stop it," I said. "She's real. You're just a memory."

"No, no, my friend. I'm not just a memory. I'm a memory with a motive. A motive provided by you."

I steeled myself and pushed my doubts aside. No. Not this time. The sadistic drug dealer wasn't going to ruin this for me.

"Goodbye, Lukas," I said while walking away. "I'm going to go enjoy myself."

"Okie dokie," he mocked. "It's too bad it's not a threesome. Those are the best. Of course you can't even be sure you are having a twosome, can you?"

His cackling followed me all the way to Bethany's bedroom, where I tried to find solace.

FRAME 6

This photograph is not like the previous five. Hackney, clothed in another thousand-dollar suit, is sitting in an overstuffed, leather office chair. This is a private moment. He's leaning forward, both feet on the floor, elbows bent on his knees, and is partially resting his head in his hands. His fingers of both hands meet to create slightly deformed pyramid, the tips of the fingers meeting at his lips. This isn't like the candid nature of the other images. The shot looks posed to me, but like it's not supposed to appear that way. While we expect phoniness from politicians, there is something false about this photo.

When asked by Metal Security, Hackney stated he didn't know when or where the photo was taken. The background of the photo is out of focus, so it's impossible to tell if the setting is an office, hotel lobby, or the inside of a home. I'm probably reading too much into it, but this doesn't look like a moment a man like Dennis Hackney would forget. Something is different about him in this shot. Something in the photo is totally, completely wrong.

Bethany was real. Or if she wasn't real, she was a hallucination I didn't want to lose. But she had to be real. I had never had a hallucination I could touch and Bethany and I certainly touched.

Lukas Derela, on the other hand, was not real anymore. We

had become acquainted during my days as a narcotics detective. He was the local leader of the group of drug dealers who abducted and tortured me for information, which I eventually gave. After my physical recovery from the ordeal, I hunted down Derela and he may or may not have come at me with a knife. Three shots to the chest later and he was in the afterlife, but unfortunately my mind has a tendency to permit inconvenient resurrections.

It turned out Derela's Pittsburgh-based gang was part of a much larger network of thugs whose members originated mostly from the former Soviet republics. Not ones to let bygones be bygones, they'd made a few attempts on my life and I'd taken out several of their members in response. Chase's concerns that the gang might take another run at me weren't unwarranted. However, I was betting they were fully aware of my extended incarceration and less aware of my release.

I told Bethany most of the story after it became apparent what we had was more than a fling. After a couple of weeks of seeing each other, she called me out on giving imprecise answers and fuzzy details concerning my life. Also, she'd met Chase by then and she got the sense he was being equally evasive, not wanting to say anything about my past that would end up wrecking our budding relationship.

Knowing full well she would eventually Google me and what kind of fallout there would be from those results, I bit the bullet and tried to ease her into the backstory. It didn't go particularly well, and she didn't speak to me for nearly a month. Much to my surprise, I didn't plummet into an emotional black hole and managed to get a job at a local furniture store. For the most part, I rode around on a truck delivering couches and dining room sets with a Puerto Rican guy named Juan who was initially frustrated with my lack of physical strength. However, the regular schedule, immersion into normal society, and manual labor had a positive effect on me. I started gaining weight and the China cabinets and oak dressers got a little lighter. My mind was clear and while not everyone I encountered was technically *real*, I developed a helpful practice of ignoring people I met along my route until Juan acknowledged them first. While the habit could make me come across as aloof, that was a reputation I was already used to carrying. From time to time, Lukas Derela and a few other dead gang members would join us on the deliveries, but I ignored them and life went on. I kept up with my weekly appointment with my psychiatrist, dutifully refilled my prescriptions, but did not take a single mind-numbing pill. If I was going to have a life, I was going to have to learn to manage my problems without the help of modern chemistry.

By the beginning of March, Bethany and I were speaking again. By the middle of the month, her apprehensiveness had waned to the point she was willing to meet me for dinner. That dinner led to another and then another until she eased into cautiously navigating the minefield of my life. Chase and I were once again on good terms and although my muscles constantly ached from heaving boxes and climbing stairs, I managed to join him in the gym once or twice per week.

March gave way to April, and on some days the thermostat rose to the point one could open windows, which was what I did as I cleaned my house on a Saturday afternoon. Bethany was coming over later in the evening and I had transformed my home from a dingy mausoleum to a respectable middle-class residence. Through my job at the furniture store, I'd acquired some slightly damaged pieces at a discounted rate. Juan was nice enough to come over and spend a weekend replacing my kitchen cabinets. He'd asked what had happened to one of the cabinet doors, but I told him it had broken off through normal wear and tear. Yep. Perfectly normal damage.

I finished straightening up in the living room and turned on the television loud enough that I'd be able to hear it while I was cooking. CNN was covering some breaking news as I walked to the kitchen to pull some ingredients out of my new, bullet-free refrigerator. A stunning African American woman sat at my kitchen table. She was in her forties and wore a blue dress and a flower in her hair. Her name was Lucile and I have no idea why I had conjured her up, but she was becoming one of my more frequent, and favorite, visitors. Lucile was humming "What a Wonderful World" by Louis Armstrong. She winked at me and I nodded to her. No reason to be rude to the non-hostile aberrations. I went about my business, which was to make oven baked chicken with rice, which is one of the four or five things I could actually cook.

The excited voice of a reporter on the television reached me in the kitchen.

...cause of the explosion is unknown at this time. Witnesses stated hearing the blast shortly after the motorcade had arrived and Mr. Hackney had entered the building with his Secret Service detail. The presidential candidate was scheduled to attend a fundraiser here at the Museum of Art in Pittsburgh and reports are Hackney was among many of those who have been transported to UPMC-Mercy Hospital.

I raced back to the living room and listened intently but the details, as they love to say on the news, were sketchy. My cell phone, which I'd finally activated, was sitting on a stand beside the front door. It started ringing and I kept my eyes glued to the television as I picked it up and answered.

"You seeing this?" asked Chase.

"Yes."

"It could be a coincidence."

"Sure."

"He's a controversial figure, Trevor. I'm sure there have been plenty of threats against him. Although the general election isn't until next year, he's such a provocative character he's already getting Secret Service protection. I'm sure they have had to filter through all sorts of threatening letters, emails, and phone calls. What Metal Security had been seeing was probably nothing in comparison."

"Right," I said as I watched footage taken from outside the

museum.

The video showed the motorcade pulling up the museum's Forbes Avenue entrance. A Secret Service agent was standing on the curb, holding his arm out as a mark for where the limo should come to a stop. During my time with Jackie, she had explained the basic protective procedures, so I recognized the agent already in place was likely the site agent who had been responsible for the advance work done on the location. Since he was the most familiar with the building, he would be the one to lead the protectee and the security detail into the site. Like clockwork, the limo pulled up far enough that the rear door was lined up perfectly with the site agent's arm and then all the cars came to a halt.

In what Jackie had taught me was a standard motorcade alignment, the procession was led by a marked police car, an unmarked Secret Service vehicle with grill lights flashing, followed by the limo. Behind the limo, there was a follow-up SUV, and then two other unmarked vehicles. When the vehicles came to a stop, the detail leader leapt out of the front seat of the limo and moved to the rear driver's side door. Agents filed out of the follow-up SUV and prepared to set up a perimeter for when Hackney exited the car. The detail leader took one last look around and then opened Hackney's door. The candidate surveyed the sidewalk, smiled, and waved at any camera he could find. He moved with his security detail up three short steps into the museum. A few seconds later, a blast could be heard and a few of the windows close to the street shattered, glass flying outward. The explosion had come from within the building.

"Are you watching CNN?" I asked.

"Of course. You know I don't watch that Fox News bullshit."

"Well, the timing of that blast can't be coincidental. That was an attack."

Neither of us spoke while we watched the footage get replayed two more times.

Finally, Chase said, "Whether he lives or dies, the Secret

Service and FBI are going to turn over every stone. Your name could come up."

I stopped watching the screen and asked "Why? That was months ago and I never did anything with the Chaerea case. This has nothing to do with me."

"I'm sure you're right, but they may still come knocking. If for no other reason, then because of the photos you claim Nick gave you."

I didn't speak. His choice of the word *claim* felt like a punch to the gut. Chase picked up on my discomfort.

"I mean the photos he gave you. Sorry."

"It's all right," I lied. "It doesn't matter. I'm sure it won't be long until someone claims responsibility or they uncover dozens of decent leads. If they get around to me at all, it won't be for weeks."

We ended the call, I turned off the television, and went back to making dinner. My friend in the kitchen was still sitting at the table, but her dress was now fire engine red. The flower was gone from her hair and she was no longer humming Louis Armstrong. Instead, she closed her eyes, leaned back in the chair, and serenaded me with a slow version of "Folsom Prison Blues."

"I'm not getting locked up again, Lucile. Stop toying with me."

She smiled and said, "Okay then, honey. I know what you need."

She stopped singing the Johnny Cash tune and immediately moved into songs of desperation and betrayal. Lucile surprised me with adding her own flare to "Someone to Watch Over Me" followed by Sheryl Crow's version of the song "The First Cut is the Deepest." What surprised me wasn't how well she performed the songs, but that she knew the lyrics. Because if she knew the words then that meant I knew the words. So kudos to me, I guess.

Bethany rang the doorbell around six. I opened the door and took her coat.

"Dinner won't be ready for few more minutes. Can I get you

a drink?"

She shrugged, still guarded around me. But she was here, which spoke volumes.

"Sure," she said. "Do you have any wine?"

Because I'd been trying to get back into shape, I hadn't been drinking much, but I had picked up a bottle of red wine because I knew it was her drink of choice.

"Of course."

"What kind?"

I hesitated and then said, "Red."

She allowed herself a giggle. "Wow. That's incredibly specific."

She had giggled. Progress.

"But it's not in a box. It's in a bottle. A glass one!"

"Wow. You really are pulling out all the stops," she took a seat on my couch and I went to get the wine.

Everything was normal. I mean there was an invisible black lady humming a Bonnie Raitt song in my kitchen, but other than that everything was normal. It felt good.

My God. *I* felt good.

FRAME 7

Citizen One was founded in 2012 as a response to the "...rising dangers of weak immigration policies accompanied by the reluctance of those entering our great nation to assimilate into American culture." While claiming to have over one million members, most hate group watch entities estimate the actual number to be less than half that amount. While even the most conservative politicians had avoided being associated with the group in previous years, the extreme views of many right-wing representatives had struck a note with a large segment of the population and ties to groups like Citizen One had become more tolerable in recent months.

An outspoken advocate of stronger immigration laws and mass deportations, Dennis Hackney found a strong following in the group and gladly accepted their invitations to speak, as well as their substantial campaign contributions. The makeshift speaking hall for the Western Pennsylvania chapter of Citizen One was a half-empty warehouse owned by Tom Linton, a member who claimed his industrial fan manufacturing business had suffered a downturn due to his competitors hiring illegals working for less than minimum wage. Linton did not view the recent steel tariffs imposed by the current administration as detrimental to his business as he did the "scourge of immigrants who are intent on weakening American values."

Hackney stood behind a flimsy-looking podium set upon a stage that appeared to be made of little more than plywood.

The photo showed Hackney, Metal Security guards on each side of the stage, and the first few rows of the crowd. Other than one of the guards, a stocky African-American woman, all the faces visible were white. Hackney's arm was extended, his finger pointing out toward the crowd. His mouth was open as if he was yelling and those in the crowd are cheering. If one did not know anything about the context of the black and white photo, one might think it had been taken at a KKK rally in the 1960s. Like the other photos, there is no exact date. But, this picture wasn't snapped during a different era. It captured a moment too close to now.

Bethany had stayed until nearly midnight. Our dinner conversation continued through dessert—a store bought apple pie—and I realized that at some point Lucile had retired from the stage for the evening. While I was open with Bethany about most of my issues, I omitted the fact I had stopped taking my pills altogether and that I spent a good amount of time with people who didn't exist. I was already keeping up the same charade with Chase by explaining my ability to concentrate had come about because my psychiatrist made adjustments in my medications. I knew he suspected I was lying, but he didn't press. While I didn't like hiding the truth from Bethany, there was only so much I could expect her to handle.

Bethany explained she wasn't ready to spend the night although I hadn't asked. I walked her out to her Toyota and we shared a passionate kiss under a streetlight. We said good night and then she got in the car and pulled away. I inhaled the chilled air and watched as my exhaled breath floated into the night. I began walking up the sidewalk toward the front porch as I became aware of eyes on me. I'd detected motion in the house to the right of mine. It was Mrs. Wellstone who I'd had cordial conversations with up to the point when I'd been arrested and become front page news. A few weeks ago I'd seen her watching the circus as the police had gone through my house so they could ultimately let me know I was a fucking loon who had imagined people impersonated police officers and interrogate me about photos I apparently never possessed. Although she was backlit, I could see the scornful expression on her face as she peeked around a lace curtain she'd probably purchased around the time of the moon landing. I should have ignored her, but I was in high spirits after my date so I winked at the old lady. She vanished in a flurry of lace and the room turned black.

I slept like the dead and decided to attack Sunday morning with a hard workout. Starting from my house, I ran three miles at a nine-minute per mile pace until I reached the Brookline Memorial Park. I cranked out two sets of fifty push-ups followed by seventy-five crunches. Using some playground equipment, I made an attempt to rattle off some pull-ups, but managed to complete only three. I still had a lot of work to do.

I did an easy run back to my street, but slowed to a walk when I saw the black Chevy Impala parked in front of my house. There were two men standing at my door and one was pressing the doorbell. The taller of the men was in khakis and a waterproof Helly Hansen jacket, thick enough to stay warm, thin enough to allow for quick movements. Beneath his slightly bent knees were scuffed hiking boots. He was standing off to the side of the door and had his left hand near a well-worn holster on his hip. The other man, who was standing centered in front of the door was in a black suit and the tops of his shoe reflected enough light to signal for a rescue aircraft. His hair was combed neatly to the side and I would have bet he had it cut every other week, come hell or high hair gel.

The guy in the Helly Hansen saw me approaching, reached over and tapped the man I knew couldn't have been his partner on the shoulder. They walked toward the street and they reached me as I made it to the puny dogwood tree on my lawn.

Pretty Boy said, "Mr. Galloway?"

They both reached into their jackets, to retrieve their credentials and badges although I had a hunch what badges I'd see. There are few things I hate more than law enforcement stereotypes, but some are damn accurate.

I pointed at Pretty Boy and said, "You're FBI."

Then, I pointed at Helly Hansen guy and said, "I'd guess you're Secret Service or ATF."

They completed their badge pulls and Pretty Boy stepped forward to take the lead.

"Yes, Mr. Galloway. I'm Special Agent Ross with the Federal Bureau of Investigation. This is Special Agent Kasper with the Secret Service. We'd like to speak with you."

I'd told Chase it would be weeks until they got around to talking to me. It had been less than twenty-four hours.

"Come on in," I said as I took a step.

Ross sidestepped into my path. "Actually, it would be better if you came—"

"That would be fine," said Kasper.

Ross did a poor job at not appearing perturbed, but bit his tongue. I retrieved a house key from something called a SPIbelt, which is essentially an elastic belt with a small pocket that can be zipped. It's like a thin fanny pack for runners, but you don't get ridiculed. The men stayed right on my heels as I opened the door, let them in, and closed it behind them.

I motioned toward my living room and said, "Have a seat if you'd like. I need a glass of water from the kitchen. Do either of you want anything?"

As I expected, neither of them wanted a drink from a person of interest nor to have a seat while the aforementioned subject moved toward a room stocked with knives and God knows what else. If these two were hallucinations, they were at least tactically aware hallucinations. Well, at least Kasper was. He slid to the entryway of the kitchen while I got myself a drink. I brought my water into the living room and took a seat in one of my two chairs. Ross followed suit and claimed the other chair. Kasper didn't even glance at the couch, but instead stood nearly opposite of me, keeping his hands in front at the ready.

"You were expecting us, Mr. Galloway," said the FBI agent.

"I was expecting someone would come knocking eventually, but not quite so soon. Hackney has been all over the news and I'm sure you need to look into anything remotely suspicious or unusual."

I'd skimmed the headlines on my computer in the morning and read that Hackney had survived the attack and his injuries were not considered to be life threatening. Several members of his Secret Service detail had received minor injuries. Amazingly, nobody had been killed in the explosion. The reporter I'd seen on television had seemed disappointed as she noted that investigators were being tight-lipped regarding any details.

"And you understand basic investigative procedure because you were a cop," said Ross.

There was something condescending in the way he said "basic," but I let it go.

"I think most people would expect that kind of reaction by law enforcement."

"But not only did you know I was in law enforcement, but you knew I was with the FBI."

"Sure."

"How did you know?"

The words *overdressed, over-groomed,* and *inadequately safety cautious* came to mind.

However, not wanting to offend, I said, "The FBI has jurisdiction if a presidential candidate is attacked."

"How would you know that? That's not something most people realize."

"As I'm sure you know, I used to be in a relationship with Special Agent Jackie Fontree." I looked over to Kasper who didn't show any reaction whatsoever.

The Secret Service isn't a big agency, so I asked Kasper, "Did you know her?"

He shook his head. "I transferred here from DC last year. I

never knew her."

"What about Nick Van Metre?" I asked.

"We crossed paths," he replied. "But that's about it."

He reached for his back pocket and produced a notepad with a pen stuck in the spirals. He flipped the cover and scribbled something on the first page.

The first page, I thought. *Either I'm their first interview or I warranted my own notebook.*

"We understand you recently had contact with Mr. Van Metre," said Kasper.

Nice, I thought. Kasper effortlessly directed the conversation by using my questions to segue to his own. Additionally, he didn't say "you *claim* to have had contact." Secret Service agents—especially those based in Washington, DC—get to spend a lot of quality time interviewing people who are schizophrenic, paranoid, delusional, or some combination thereof since a lot of threats against protectees are made by people with less-than-optimal psychological histories. My guess is Kasper wasn't picked at random to come speak with me. He was probably highly-experienced in working on what the agency calls protective intelligence cases. Not only did I warrant the first page of his notebook, but a personal appearance by a protective intelligence expert.

Yay.

I took a drink from my glass. I was still sweating some from my run, so hopefully these guys didn't think their presence was making me nervous. Maybe I should have been nervous, but since I had put Nick Van Metre, Metal Security, and Dennis Hackney in the rearview mirror quite a while ago, there was nothing to worry about.

"Nick came by a while back and asked me to help him with a possible threat case. I thought about it, but decided I wouldn't be much help," I said.

"So, he was recruiting you?" asked Kasper.

I shrugged. Started to speak, but paused when I thought I

heard something coming from the kitchen.

"Mr. Galloway?"

"Yes," I said, turning my attention back to Kasper. "I guess you could say that."

"What exactly did Mr. Van Metre ask you to do?"

I explained my conversation with Nick, the email from Chaerea, and the photographs.

"Do you still have these photographs?" said the FBI man.

"No. I threw them away when I decided to decline the case."

"So, you don't have any proof that these photographs existed?"

"Nick told me he had the original photos."

"At his house?" said the FBI agent.

At his house? Weird question. *Why would Nick have them at his house?*

"I have no idea," I said. "I assumed at his office." Then it hit me. "Are the original photos missing?"

"Let's move on," said Kasper.

The original photos were missing, I thought. *Nick called in a break-in at his house in the days before he was killed, but then told the police to disregard. Why? Maybe it was because he realized the photos had been the target and were missing. But why keep them at home and not in a safe at the office? What the hell were you up to, Nick?*

"Do you have any emails from Mr. Van Metre?" Kasper asked.

"No. They disap—I don't have them anymore."

A moment of quiet overtook the room, but the sound of the noise coming from the kitchen increased. Lucile. Goddamn Lucile and her humming.

Kasper nodded and didn't betray an ounce of disbelief.

Then he said, "We were told two visitors came by and asked about Mr. Van Metre as well as the photographs and that some sort of disturbance ensued."

The humming got louder. What was she humming? Something

by Elvis again. She loved Elvis tunes.

"Right," I said. "Well, as I'm sure you are aware, I have a colorful psychiatric history."

"So, you don't believe those visitors were real?" the FBI man chimed in.

I was at a crossroads. I was sixty percent sure the police impersonators had been real. Maybe fifty-five percent. However, if I admitted as much then these guys would be one hundred percent sure I was crazy.

"I was late taking my meds that day and hadn't been sleeping well," I said. "There was no evidence those people were real."

Kasper stepped forward and asked, "How is your grip on reality right now?"

"Stellar," I replied as Lucile hummed away.

"Do you feel confident we are actually here?" he asked.

"Yes."

"What medications are you on?"

Kasper scribbled in his notepad as I gave him the names of the drugs and the dosages I should have been taking.

Ross jumped in and, with the subtlety of sandpaper, said, "Mr. Galloway. As you alluded, we have done some research on you so we know a bit about your background. You are telling us that Nick Van Metre, the former partner of Jackie Fontree who was killed in the course of an investigation in which you were involved, offered to bring you—a man who had a psychotic break—in on a case to protect a man running for president of the United States. You have no proof of this, but claim to have at one time been in possession of a cryptic threatening email and a packet of photographs. Additionally, you're on record stating two individuals impersonated police officers and tried to get information from you. In fact, the official incident report states you said one of the impersonators took a shot at you."

I waited. My eyes shifted to Kasper. I could see in his face that this wasn't good cop, bad cop. Kasper was annoyed at the FBI man's clumsiness.

Ross continued, "One might think you have delusions of grandeur, a strong desire to be involved in a case of national importance, and a touch of paranoia. You may not know this, but the explosion that injured Dennis Hackney was no accident. Someone tried to kill him with an improvised explosive device and—I can't tell you how—but the name Chaerea has come up during the investigation. You are the only person linked to that name. Now, as an agent of the FBI, what am I supposed to do with that?"

I looked at him and said, "Well, if my experience with the Bureau has taught me anything, you'll wait for another agency to solve the case and then call a press conference to take credit."

I'm not certain, but I think I heard Kasper stifle a laugh. Ross was less amused and his cheeks flushed.

The humming got louder and I could almost identify the song.

Kasper interjected to smooth things over. "We have no reason to believe you are involved, Mr. Galloway. But, perhaps you might have information that could assist the investigation."

Kasper was approaching this as an intelligence gathering operation while Ross had come in looking at things through the lens of a criminal investigator. Being adversarial can be counter-productive when gathering intel, especially if the subject of the investigation is unstable. For Kasper and the Secret Service, the first priority was to identify the threat and prevent another attack. Prosecution was secondary. For Ross, prosecution was the primary purpose and headlines were second. In truth, I had sympathy for the FBI. In recent years they had been pulled into politics and accused of being part of a deep state conspiracy against a president. Of course, most people knew that was all nonsense. The FBI has thousands of employees who, like all the other federal law enforcement agencies, serve both Republican and Democrat administrations. The deep state theory was nothing more than a desperate Hail Mary thrown by cornered politicians. But, still—Ross was kind of a dick.

"What would you like to know, Agent Kasper? I assume you

want to go over my employment history, drug and alcohol use, support structure to include relationships with family and friends, special interests in any political matters, access to weapons, and my ability to organize and carry out a plan."

Kasper grinned. "That's the gist of it. But let's get the ugly stuff out of the way. Where were you at the time of explosion?"

"Right here," I said. "In fact my friend Detective Chase Vinson of the Pittsburgh PD called me when he saw it on the news. I received the call on my cell phone, so I'm sure records will show the call bounced off a tower here somewhere."

He scribbled in the notebook. "That's good. As you can guess, we'd like to search your house in order to help exclude you as a suspect. Do you have any weapons in the house or anything else we should know about?"

That question was starting to become the most popular one in Pittsburgh.

"No."

"Would you consent to a search?"

"Knock yourself out."

Kasper nodded. I glanced at his FBI counterpart. Judging from Ross's expression, he wasn't expecting that answer.

He leapt up from his chair with more enthusiasm than necessary and said, "You can stay with Mr. Galloway and collect all the background information your people need. I'll check the house."

Kasper sighed softly and kept writing in his notes.

When Ross left the room to start his search in the kitchen, I said, "So I have a reasonable alibi unless the IED was on a timer."

Kasper watched me, but didn't reveal anything.

"How did the name Chaerea pop up? Did someone claim credit?"

He watched me, but didn't reveal anything.

Ross came out of the kitchen and started moving to the staircase.

Since the FBI man was in earshot, I said to Kasper, "So since

I wasn't there I couldn't have done it."

Ross stopped, turned and said, "The bomb in the air intake vent was on a timer Mr. Galloway. Someone knew when Hackney was going to arrive and that he was supposed to stop in the hallway and meet with some VIPs. Fortunately, Mr. Hackney took longer in the hallway than what was on the event schedule. You aren't in the clear for anything."

Ross continued up the stairs and I watched as Kasper rolled his eyes.

"You might as well tell me," I said. "If he doesn't spill all the details now, he'll leak it to the press by this afternoon."

Kasper took a seat in the chair vacated by Ross. "Let's just go over your background information."

"The FBI must have been thrilled to have the Secret Service tag along. How's that working out?"

Kasper flashed a wry smile. "We all have crosses to bear, Mr. Galloway. Let's talk about some of yours."

We spent the better part of the next hour reexamining my life and recounting my limited affiliation with Nick Van Metre and Metal Security. Ross finished digging through my belongings returned to pace impatiently while Kasper finished up the interview.

"I think that covers everything for now, Mr. Galloway. I've got your phone number should we have any more questions."

Ross excitedly moved in and said, "I have a few more questions for you. Our understanding is you once—"

"Agent Ross," I interrupted. "I think Agent Kasper and I covered everything. Maybe you'll get something from the phone call you received from Chaerea when he or she claimed credit for the attack."

Ross said, "The call? You mean the note at the scene?"

I turned back to Kasper who dipped his head and closed his eyes. Ross picked up on the fact he'd revealed a detail they probably planned on withholding from the press and the redness returned to his face.

Kasper stood. "Time to go. Thank you for your cooperation, Mr. Galloway."

I walked both men to the door and made sure to shake hands with each of them. The skin-to-skin contact was reassuring and not-so-reassuring. These were real people. This was actually happening—which had its upside and obvious downside. I closed the door and peered out the small window in the entryway.

Once the federal agents reached the Impala, I said, "Stop it, Lucile. It's not funny."

I had finally placed the Elvis song she was humming.

It was "Jailhouse Rock."

FRAME 8

From the looks of it, Dennis Hackney's arrival at Allegheny General Hospital was not a quiet one. The photographer was positioned in the lobby and snapped the picture before Hackney passed through a glass door being held open by a member of his Metal Security team. In the background, a group of demonstrators were holding signs and appeared to be chanting. Unlike most of the other photos, the background is clear enough to read the words scrawled on poster board.

CONVERSION THERAPY IS TORTURE
LOVE IS MY RELIGION

Separate from the other signs, one woman stood alone with a square of poster board larger than the others. She held the sign high above her head, her eyes filled with rage and resolve.

A RECKONING IS COMING

Metal Security had expected an increase in demonstrations like this one. Not long after he announced his candidacy, an online magazine had unearthed a video recording of Hackney and his wife at a benefit. The two were standing with another couple and Hackney was recorded uttering homophobic slurs. The discussion had reportedly involved the subject of gay marriage, an idea Hackney opposed fervently. The other couple, and Hackney's wife, Vanessa, appeared uncomfortable during the rant, but had stopped short of arguing with the millionaire who was used to bending others to his will.

As he entered the hospital, his expression was one of defiance and annoyance. I counted two other security personnel in the photo and someone I assumed was a representative of the hospital was waiting inside the lobby to greet him. Hackney was there to tour their new cardiology center, a project to which he had made large contributions. Initially he had demanded the center be named after him, but hospital administrators had refused once Hackney's homophobic comments had been picked up by the mainstream media. Rather than get labeled as being petty by the liberal media machine he was convinced was conspiring against him, he did not demand the hospital return his contribution. The cardiac center may not get named after him, but he'd be damned if he wouldn't use it as a good photo op.

Three days after my interview with Ross and Kasper, my peaceful employment at the furniture store hit a slight speed bump. Juan and I had finished loading a coffee table into the back of a truck when my cell phone chimed. It was a text message from Chase that read, *Visitors on their way to you. I gave them your work location. Been told to stay clear due to possible conflict of interest. They know you by rep. Not in a good way.*

Since the feds already knew where I worked, I assumed somebody from the Pittsburgh PD was headed my way. Everyone in the department knew Chase and I were close, so it wasn't surprising he'd been told to keep his distance. It was unlikely the city would want to get in the way of the federal investigation regarding Hackney, who according to the news had been released from the hospital, so that meant the department had decided to talk to me about Nick's murder. Fortunately, I had plenty of practice answering questions about that case, since I'd already been interviewed by two police impersonators who nobody else believed existed. I was fifty percent sure those two really existed. Maybe forty-five.

Not wanting there to be any kind of public scene that would jeopardize my employment, I found the store manager in his office and told him the police were coming to interview me because a friend of mine had been killed. I let him know the cops wanted to get some background information so they could try to determine who may have wanted to hurt him. Nick wasn't exactly a friend and I suspected the police wanted a little more than background information, but I wanted to sugarcoat the situation as much as possible.

Twenty minutes later, two detectives arrived at the store and identified themselves to Bob, who was working the sales floor. Demetrius, a twenty-something who apparently had watched too many episodes of *The Wire*, came into the stockroom wide-eyed after seeing the investigators flash shields, found me, and whispered that the *Five-O* were out front asking for me.

"Okay," I whispered back, emphasizing the O.

I walked out on the showroom floor and noticed the detectives were standing beside a sectional sofa.

Bob, a frail man in his sixties, twitched his mustache and jutted a thumb in the direction of the detectives.

"They'd like to talk to you."

The portly one with the shaved head and goatee reached into a pocket of his navy-blue cargo pants and retrieved a cell phone. He snapped a photo of the couch and said something to his partner, who could have passed for his brother if he'd told his barber to ditch the clippers for a straight razor. They turned simultaneously as I approached.

"Detectives," I said.

I didn't bother introducing myself. Most of the department either knew me or had seen photos of me in the newspaper.

The one with the shaved head said, "First question: What do you call this kind of couch?"

I shrugged and said, "Heavy."

Neither of the detectives smiled, reminding me that I'm not funny.

"I just carry the things, but I'm happy to get Bob or Demetrius. Either one of them can tell you all about the furniture."

"Demetrius?" The one with the buzz cut asked, "Is that the squirmy kid who rushed off to find you?"

"Yes."

"He started sweating as soon as we flashed our badges. What's his deal?"

"Too much television," I said.

"I'm Detective Bryan Langdale." He gestured to his short-haired companion. "This is Detective Gerchak. We were hoping you'd take a ride with us so we can speak privately."

I looked around the room. It was totally empty and I imagined Demetrius was busy calling his *homies* who undoubtedly lived near him in upper-middle-class Wexford. My guess was he would be spinning a tale of how he pulled one over on the cops because they didn't notice his maroon company polo shirt smelled like weed—which it always did.

"This seems private enough," I said, waving a hand to point out the empty showroom.

Langdale put a hand on my shoulder and said, "Come on. We just want to clear some things up about your connection to Nick Van Metre."

I didn't like him touching me. I didn't like it at all.

"Here is fine," I said.

He squeezed a little harder and said, "We understand you thought some of our people already spoke with you about this, but we can assure you *we* are real and extremely interested in your story. It's not like you've had trouble talking before. Remember when you gave up all those names to your drug dealer buddies?"

"Please take your hand off me," I said.

He didn't.

Gerchak stepped in and I thought he might tell his partner to back off.

He didn't.

"Didn't Nick Van Metre work with your former girlfriend? What was her name...Janice...no, Jackie. That's it. Jackie Fontree. Do you think they ever had a thing? We were thinking maybe Van Metre *did* actually come see you and maybe he wasn't too crazy about you helping to get Jackie killed. The word is, her investigation had been going pretty well until you got involved."

"She got burned on surveillance," I said. "That wasn't my doing."

"But you changed the course of that entire case, didn't you?" said Gerchak. "The after action reports stated the targets became more vigilant because you were sniffing around. You took everyone to DEFCON 1 and blood got spilled."

Langdale squeezed harder and his thumb pressed on a soft spot above my collar bone. I knew what they were trying to do. It was no secret that I used to have a temper and if they could provoke me into assaulting a police officer then they could take me into custody. Once I was in custody, they would try to get me into an interrogation room. Or if that didn't work and I lawyered up, maybe they would take me in for a mandatory psychiatric evaluation. I didn't find either of these options appealing.

"Detectives, I have a confession to make."

They both leaned in. I looked around as if checking to see that nobody could overhear.

"You know how I said Nick Van Metre came to see me?"

"Yeah," they said at the same time.

I paused for effect.

"It was a hallucination."

They leaned back and scowled.

"But, I'm doing better now and I'm not a threat to myself or others. Now, I'm not under arrest. There is no cause to take me in for a psych eval. And I still have the number of the lawyer who was good enough to get me a deal for a stint in a psychiatric treatment center after I committed multiple homicides."

Langdale released his grip.

We locked eyes for a moment. I'd hoped my words would get them to back off, but they seemed to have had the opposite effect. Both men squeezed in close and I braced myself for violence. Then a bell chimed as the front door to the store opened. I glanced and did a double-take.

"Hey, sweetie! Sorry I'm a few minutes early."

Early?

Bethany strode across the floor, maneuvering between two staged bedrooms, and stood on her toes to give me a kiss.

Before I could speak, she said, "Introduce me to your friends."

I stammered, "These are Detectives Gerchak and Langdale."

Bethany extended a hand. The men seemed taken aback, but shook her hand in turn.

"Did the three of you work together in the department?"

I didn't answer, so Langdale rubbed a hand over his smooth head and said, "No, ma'am. We heard Mr. Galloway may have known a man who was murdered, so we stopped by to see if he has any insights."

Bethany smiled, but I knew her well enough to know it wasn't a true smile.

"Well, you picked the right consultant," she said. "Not only did he solve the Peter Lanskard homicide a few years ago, but he cracked the Jimmy Spartan homicide that you guys never could."

I hadn't gone into those cases with her, but apparently Bethany had spent the past few weeks doing her own research.

"Tell me about the case you guys are working on now?" she asked excitedly. "It must be a tough one if you need Trevor's help."

The two men shifted uncomfortably.

Gerchak said, "We really can't go into it now." Then, to me he said, "Thank you for your help, Mr. Galloway. We'll be in touch."

He said that last part with a trace of a growl.

I waited until the men were out of the store and then I turned to Bethany.

"What are you doing here? I didn't know you were coming by."

Now her smile was genuine.

"I'm your backup."

"Backup? How did...," I stopped myself from asking the question as the only reasonable answer slapped me upside the head. "Chase," I said. "Chase called you."

"He said he'd been told to stay away, so he asked if I could stop by to see how things were going. I wasn't supposed to intervene unless things became adversarial, but from the looks of things when I walked in, the conversation was not a friendly one."

"Chase has your phone number?" I asked.

"He tracked it down. He said he knows the manager at the Applebee's where I work, so he got my number from him. Weird coincidence, huh?"

It wasn't really. There were three hundred thousand people in Pittsburgh and it was a safe bet Chase knew two-thirds of them.

"Chase said he knew the detectives who were coming down here and that—and I quote—'What they lack in subtlety they make up for in stupidity'."

"Thank you. Thank you for coming down here. You didn't have to do that."

"Were they asking about Dennis Hackney?"

"No. They're working Nick Van Metre's homicide."

"You told me a little about all this, but maybe it's time you told me everything."

I weighed her words. *Everything* could be a lot, but if I was going to have any shot at having a relationship with Bethany, then I needed to open up more than I had thus far.

"You obviously did some research. Are you sure you want to know more about the cases? There were...complications," I said.

She shook her head.

"Not just about the cases. I said I want to know everything. Even the stuff you're not telling anyone else."

My heart sank. Here is where I was going to lose her. If I didn't tell her I was crazy, then I'd be lying by omission. If I told her, then she'd have no choice but to stay away.

"It's going to make you leave," I said.

She reached up, put her hands on my shoulders, and looked me in the eyes. "I researched you online, Trevor."

"I figured you would eventually."

"No," she said. "I read up on you two weeks ago."

Now I got it. She had done some research, seen much of the ugliness and was still here. She had still come to my home and spent time with me. She had still kissed me.

"I don't know where to start," I said honestly.

"Well," she said. "Let's talk about how on the morning after we first met, you were talking to a dead guy in my kitchen."

FRAME 9

The landscaping behind Dennis Hackney's mansion rivaled that of a Roman emperor's. For the first time, the photograph captured not only Hackney, but a large portion of his surroundings. The neat rows of shrubbery created a maze dotted with sculptures and fountains. Stone benches had been placed along the brick path surrounding the maze and Hackney sat on the one nearest the house. Lamps designed to simulate torches illuminated large swaths of the boxwoods and juniper hedges. For once, Hackney was wearing jeans with a casual button-down shirt. The Metal Security notes state the photo was taken late in the evening. At the edge of where a shadow met light, Hackney was lighting a cigarette. He was not wearing a coat, indicating the evening was unseasonably warm or perhaps he decided to brave the chill long enough to get his nicotine fix.

The darkness intruded along the borders of the maze, but one could make out something near a dogwood tree. At first glance one might have assumed it was a sculpture of warrior or statesman, but it was a man and he appeared to be walking away from Hackney. His face wasn't visible, but there was something familiar about his stature.

My phone woke me at six the next morning. I barely got a chance to clear my throat before Chase started talking.

"The pricks dropped your name to the press."

"Who?" I asked, although I would have known the answer already had I been more awake.

"Langdale and Gerchak. They leaked your name as being a possible suspect in the Van Metre murder."

"Shit."

They had no evidence of my involvement and no clear motive. I could have spent the next few minutes bemoaning my bad fortune to Chase, but what good would it do? Chase knew the deal. The detectives didn't like me and they wanted me to be as uncomfortable as possible. So here we were.

"Uh-huh. You gotta move."

Chase's sense of urgency wasn't necessarily paranoia. For most people, it would be problematic to have your name appear in the paper as part of a homicide investigation. For me, there were other considerations.

"Did you hear me?" Chase asked. "You can stay with me if you want. I may not be off the radar, but I'm not in the center of it either."

"I've been dormant for over two years. It's possible this won't matter."

Chase sighed and said, "You can't take that chance. When the EEDC realizes you're out and about, they may send hitters. You have to vaporize and I mean right now."

"The EEDC?"

"Yeah."

I waited. He didn't speak, so I had to ask.

"What the hell is the EEDC?"

"The Eastern European Drug Cartel," said Chase.

The drug gang that captured and then hunted me never had a name. That was part of their power and how they had remained relatively anonymous throughout the rust belt. It seemed *someone* had decided to name them to take away that power.

"Who came up with that name?"

"I did," said Chase with a trace of pride. "It's simple, elegant, and right to the point."

"It sounds like a boy band."

"It does not!" he said defensively.

"Or maybe an old rap group," I suggested. "Are their fugitive members called Run-EEDC?"

"Shut up! If you wanted to name them then you should have done it a long time ago. I'm sticking with EEDC."

"Suit yourself," I surrendered.

There was a pause and then Chase said, "You have another problem too."

Other than being a person of interest in the attempted assassination of a politician, a suspect in a homicide, and potentially a target of a gang of drug dealing thugs who were going to be pissed when they found out they were going to get confused with New Kids on the Block, things were going fine, so I couldn't imagine what else he was going to drop in my lap.

"What?"

"You aren't alone anymore."

I felt sick. He was right. I'd gone over to Bethany's apartment after work and we'd talked for a couple of hours. I'd given her the rundown of what had been going on with me and how Lukas Derela, Lucile, and a host of others peppered my reality. I thought she might kick me out right then and there, but she listened, asked questions, and at one point pulled out a notebook and started writing.

When I asked what she was doing she said, "I care about you Trevor and I don't know where this is going. But, one thing is for certain. You are a *gold mine* when it comes to material for a future novel."

I don't laugh out loud, but I came fairly close at that moment. In truth, she didn't absorb all of the details of my past in stride. I'd told her all about my previous run-ins with the gang, which she took better than I had anticipated. The one incident that alarmed her the most was a time I had thought I was being followed by hallucinations which had actually turned out to be a hitters for the gang. If not for a series of fortunate events, I would have taken a bullet to the head. I explained that I often couldn't distinguish between hallucinations and real people which made picking up surveillance especially difficult.

After chewing on a thumbnail, she raised her eyes and said, "From here on out, I'm your second set of eyes and your sixth sense. Nothing is getting past me, Galloway."

It sounded great at the time, and I truly thought, or hoped, the business with the gang was all in the past. But with this new threat, maybe she needed to keep her distance from me.

"I'll talk to Bethany right now," I said. "Do any of the media reports mention where I work?"

"I don't think so," said Chase.

"Then, I'll pack a bag now and head over to your place after I finish my shift. Do you think Cujo will mind?"

"He'll deal with it," said Chase of his perpetually moody Chihuahua.

"Okay. I'll see you tonight."

I started to end the call, but then realized something.

"Hey, wait."

"What?" asked Chase.

"It's six in the morning. You never get up this early, so how did you know my name hit the news?"

"Dude, I have half a dozen alerts set up to notify me if your name pops up in print."

"How long have you had that?"

"About three and a half years, I guess."

"Chase," I said.

"Yeah."

"You're a good friend."

"I know."

"But you suck at naming drug gangs and dogs."

Chase ended the call. I started to dial Bethany, but decided the matter was best discussed in person. So, I rushed through my morning routine, packed a bag, and drove over to her apartment while doing my best to make sure I wasn't followed. I hated waking her up, but I knew she would be more understanding of the news if I presented it face to face.

"Nope."

"I don't think you understand," I said.

Bethany rubbed her eyes and walked into the kitchen, so I followed. She yawned and started preparing coffee.

"If they come for me," I explained, "they won't care if you get hurt or killed. In fact, they would brutalize you just to make me suffer. These people are relentless."

She retrieved two coffee mugs from a drying rack beside the sink, paused and whispered, "Should I get a mug for Lukas?"

"This is serious," I said.

She placed the mugs on the table and sat down. I took the chair across from her.

"I'm not *completely* sold on you yet, but I'm not staying away from you," she said. "So...no."

For someone who always appears stern, I was doing a terrible job of conveying the risk associated with being near me. I had to make certain she understood this wasn't her choice and that I wasn't making a request. I didn't want to hurt her and while it was going to kill me to push her away, I couldn't let anything happen to her because of my past.

"I'm sorry," I said. "This is the way it has to be."

"Nope."

"Bethany, I'm not asking. I have to lay low."

She leaned back and crossed her bare legs. This morning she was wearing a long T-shirt that read, *Not my circus. Not my monkeys.*

"And I'm supposed to go on with my life as if you don't exist? Or maybe you're expecting I'm going to sit here in this apartment, chew on my nails, and wait for Chase to call to tell me you're dead. Or, maybe these people, the..."

"EEDC," I said. "Eastern European Drug Cartel."

"That's a stupid name."

"I know," I agreed.

"Or maybe this EEDC already knows about me and you think I'm going to wait around for them to abduct me in an effort to draw you out. Then you'll come out of hiding and valiantly rescue the young and naïve damsel in distress. Are those the scenarios you were envisioning?"

"I…no, it's just that—"

"They come for you, then they come for us," she said.

"I can't let that happen, Bethany."

"You don't have a choice, Trevor. If these guys are as evil as you say, then there is the possibility they've been biding their time and waiting to make sure federal agents or local police aren't watching you. They may have already decided that you're too hot right now and that killing me is the best way to hurt you."

Crap.

She stood, retrieved the coffee pot and poured our coffee.

"Sorry, dear," she said. "One team, one fight."

She replaced the coffee pot, turned, took a sip, and gave me a wink. Now I knew without a doubt that she was in harm's way. I knew it because I was falling in love with her.

FRAME 10

The Pennsylvania Coal Conglomerate's annual meeting in Monroeville usually slipped past anything other than the local media outlets. This time, the presence of a presidential hopeful pushed the gathering of those representing two hundred thirty companies tied to the state's troubled coal industry into the national spotlight. Hackney had one hand on a railing and was ascending makeshift stairs leading up to a stage constructed at the front of the banquet hall. As a major investor in several energy companies, Hackney had joined in with others who declared there was a "war on coal" and advocated for a reduction in environmental regulations.

Nothing stands out in the photograph, other than it was taken from below stage level and from the side. Hackney must have walked right past the photographer. Hackney is there. Metal Security guards are flanking the stage. The crowd and press pool are where one would expect. It's all there, except what is not.

Nearly a week passed and, other than my sleeping on Chase's couch, life went on as if Nick Van Metre had never darkened my doorway and Dennis Hackney was simply another talking head one mutes when he's on TV. Of course, I knew some people were questioning if Nick really had reached out to me or if I'd dreamed up the entire story about Dennis Hackney, Chaerea, and the photographs. While I was relieved that a brigade of

Lithuanian and Estonian drug dealers didn't descend on me once my name started circulating, I worried Bethany would become complacent as we maintained our daily routines. So far, she had stayed vigilant and helped keep my mind at ease by calling me before going in to work her shift tending bar.

"I think someone is watching my apartment."

I wasn't certain I heard correctly, since I was surrounded by barking dogs and nervous cats. Chase had to work, but it was my day off and he had asked me if I could take Cujo to a vet appointment. The four-pound ball of maliciousness didn't care for me any more than I cared for him, so it was no small favor to ask. However, there I was sitting in the vet's waiting room with a Chihuahua named after a giant dog of Stephen King's creation when Bethany had called.

I pressed the phone hard against my ear and asked her to repeat what she'd said.

"I'm looking out the window and there's a green Buick parked half a block down. I think there are two people in it and they've been there at least twenty minutes."

"And you don't remember seeing the car before?" I asked.

"Pretty much everyone in my building is under fifty. I think I'd remember seeing a Buick. Nobody drives a Buick except old people."

"I don't think that's true."

"Really? Name one Buick owner you know who doesn't collect social security."

The sounds of a dispute between a black lab and a labradoodle filled the void left by my silence.

"I'm going to go out the back to get a better look at them."

"What? No, don't do that!" I said. "Call the police and tell them there is a suspicious car outside your apartment building and that you think you may be in danger."

"What if it is the cops? Maybe they're watching me because of my connection to you."

The thought had occurred to me.

"Then, no harm no foul."

I pulled Cujo by the leash and tugged him toward the exit. He grumbled an objection as his tiny feet slid across the tile floor. The little bastard made me drag him into the veterinarian's office building and now he was making me drag him the other way.

"Bethany?"

She didn't respond, but I heard the jingle of keys.

"Bethany. Don't go out there!"

"I'm just going to take a quick look. I at least want to be able to recognize them if I see them again. I can't see their faces from my apartment window."

Now I was rushing with Cujo toward my car. He was finally cooperating.

"No, stay!" I said to Bethany.

Cujo sat.

"I'll be discreet," Bethany said.

"Go!" I said to Cujo.

"I'm already going," said Bethany. "I'm already walking down the back staircase."

"No, not you!" I said. "I'm talking to Cujo. I want *you* to stay!"

Cujo sat.

"Godammit!" I yelled.

"Don't yell at me," she said.

I took a deep breath and spoke slowly. "Can you just wait? I'll be there in ten minutes."

"Sure," she said as I heard the telltale sound of the crash bar of a door being pressed.

Cujo snarled as I picked him up and put him in the back seat of my Volkswagen. I jumped in the driver's seat and started the engine.

"You're already outside, aren't you?" I asked.

"Yeah, I'll call you back."

"No don't—" I began. But she'd already ended the call.

I dialed her number while I drove to her place, but the call went to voice mail. I started to dial 9-1-1, but stopped when I realized I might be overreacting. So what if someone in a Buick was parked outside Bethany's building? It could be someone visiting a tenant. It could have been someone interested in renting an apartment. It could have been someone picking up a friend or relative. The number of harmless possibilities outnumbered the threatening ones. It's not like Bethany was trained to recognize surveillance. The woman had a degree in literature from Clarion University and had never even studied criminal justice, much less gone through actual training. She had no idea what she was looking at and her overactive writer's imagination was probably getting the best of her. The chances were good I was going to pull up to find her sitting on a park bench while covertly peeking around the edge of a newspaper as if she was a character in a bad spy novel. My heart rate had slowed and my thoughts had calmed by the time I turned the corner onto the street in front of Bethany's apartment. My stomach leapt into my throat as I noticed a crowd gathered in the street near a green Buick.

I screeched up to the scene, causing Cujo to fall onto the floor of the back seat. He growled at me as I jumped out of the car and pushed my way through the crowd. As I neared the car, I saw a woman slumped on the ground, leaning back against one of the tires. She was covering her face and blood was visible around her hands. Then, I saw a flash of motion near the woman's feet and saw Bethany was beating the hell out of a man who was doing his best to cover his face and body as she delivered punch after punch. I rushed over, grabbed Bethany from behind, and pulled her off the bearded man who immediately slinked back and took up a position next to the woman I presumed had been with him in the car.

"What the hell are you doing?" I said to Bethany, spinning her around.

She was laboring to catch her breath, but said, "They spotted me and tried to act like they didn't recognize me, but it was clear they did. So, I yanked open the driver's door and asked him what they were doing. They got evasive and then I really started looking at them and remembered you had described them to me."

"I described them to you? What on earth are you talking about?"

I let her go and looked down at the two bloodied figures sitting on the street.

"My God," I said.

"Yeah," said Bethany.

Bleeding there on the asphalt were two people I thought I'd never see again. In fact, I had started to think I'd never met them at all.

I stood over them and said, "I'm not sure what to call you, but I'm guessing detectives Elisa Hayes and Lincoln Bayless probably aren't the names that you'll be booked under."

I reached down to them and searched them for weapons. I pulled FN Five-Seven pistols off each of them and held one in each hand. The guns weren't peashooters. The Five-Seven was capable of firing 5.7x28mm rounds, which meant the weapon had major penetrating power. Some varieties of the ammunition weren't even available to civilians because the rounds could easily penetrate ballistic vests. Some in the media and in law enforcement had designated bullets of that variety *cop killers*.

The small crowd that had gathered backed up and scattered, deciding gunplay was less amusing than watching an attractive redhead pummel people on the street. I'd left my cellphone in the car so I turned to Bethany and asked if she still had her phone. She retrieved it from the back pocket of her jeans and held it up.

"Call the cops and tell them we have two armed police impersonators down here."

"Wait," said the woman. "You don't want to do that."

"Sure, I do," I said. "You tried to kill me and I tend to hold grudges when it comes to things like that."

I nodded to Bethany and said, "Go ahead."

The woman on the ground spoke up again and said, "And what exactly do you think they are going to arrest us for? We don't know you. We've never met you. We were sitting here, minding our own business, when this psycho bitch attacked us. There are plenty of witnesses, so if anyone is getting locked up, it's her."

The man I knew as Detective Bayless spoke quietly and added, "I wonder how the cops are going to react to the infamous Trevor Galloway taking our legally owned guns away while threatening our lives."

"I never threatened you," I said.

"We say you did," he replied. "You were talking nonsense about us impersonating police officers and following your girlfriend around. Of course, this is all a big shock to us. We're two law-abiding citizens who are going to have to testify at your commitment hearing."

I had to admit, for a man who wasn't bleeding and was holding two guns, my confidence level was suddenly piss poor.

"Trevor," said Bethany. "I don't mind being arrested for assault. I'll take my chances."

I knew an assault charge wouldn't be the end of the world for her, but Bayless and Hayes—or whatever their real names might be—were right. I had nothing on them. Maybe their guns were legal, maybe they weren't. But, it was true that an identification made by Trevor Galloway was less than worthless and my standing in the street holding a couple of Five-Sevens was exactly what the real Pittsburgh detectives, Langdale and Gerchak, needed to have me tossed into jail or a psychiatric ward.

"Who are you?" I asked.

The bearded man got to his feet and said, "Who we are isn't important. But, our employer would like to speak with you."

"Who do you work for?"

He shook his head. "Come with us and find out."

"There's no way I'm getting in a car with you."

He held out his hands in a conciliatory gesture. Blood still ran from his nose. "Feel free to follow in your own car." He looked at Bethany who was still frozen with the phone in her hands. "You're both invited, of course."

Bethany put the phone away and stepped forward. "So you came here to arrange a meeting, not kill us?"

"That is correct. We simply didn't know if Mr. Galloway was here."

"Do you always follow orders?" I asked him.

"Yes."

I struck him across the face with the gun I was holding in my right hand. He staggered back and nearly lost his balance. He gathered himself and stared me down.

"Then I had nothing to lose by doing that," I said. "I'll follow you."

"We'll follow you," Bethany corrected.

I started to protest, but she cut me off.

"It's happening. They know where I live and I'm the one they were watching. I'm invested, so deal with it."

I wanted to argue, but I could hear sirens in the distance. It was likely one of the bystanders had called the police once the guns came out.

"Our weapons," said Bayless.

He moved forward and held out his hands.

"Oh," I said. "Here you go."

This time I hit him in the face with the gun I was holding in my left hand.

"You son of a bitch," he yelled as he leaned over and held his face.

"I'll keep the guns. Get in your car and start driving. If we don't like where we're going, we drive away and the whole thing is off. We'll take our chances with the cops."

"Fine," he said.

The fake detectives got into their car and Bethany and I did the same. I tucked the guns under my seat while Bethany was greeted by an enthusiastic Cujo, who liked her a hell of a lot more than he liked me.

"Want to leave him in my apartment?" she said.

"There's no time," I said. "It sounds like someone called the police."

"Do you think this is a good idea?"

"No," I said.

"But we're going anyway."

"Right."

"And why is that?" she asked.

"First, because I don't want either of us to get arrested. Second, because this may be a once in a lifetime opportunity for you."

"How do you figure?"

The Buick pulled into traffic. I put my Jetta into gear and followed.

"Because I think the person you're about to meet may end up being the president of the United States."

FRAME 11

The dinner cruise on the Gateway Clipper was an opportunity for those who peddle influence to mingle with those with deep pockets. The fifteen hundred-dollar-per-plate, two-hour event took guests up and down Pittsburgh's three rivers, the Allegheny, the Monongahela, and the Ohio. Three Pennsylvania congressmen and several state representatives flanked Dennis Hackney as he stood at the end of the glassed-in dining room nearest the bow. Two Metal Security representatives can be seen in the background as well as two staff members I've come to recognize from other photos. While the faces of the Metal Security employees change, the staffers remain the same. They are the constants in the equation and would have to be scrutinized should there be any kind of attack on Hackney that would require coordination or timing. Other than security personnel and Hackney himself, they are the ones who know his schedule and help guide him into and out of events. But for some reason the constants don't bother me as much as the variables. Variables are what you don't account for and variables are what will get you killed.

"Why do you think they are taking us to see Dennis Hackney?" Bethany asked.

"First, can we discuss how stupid it was for you to get into a physical confrontation with those two? You could have been killed!"

She held Cujo in her lap and he glared at me as I yelled. As I expected, Bayless and Hayes entered I-279 and began leading us north of downtown.

"Okay, okay. Not my best moment. I was going to get a description of them and maybe snap a quick photo with my phone, but then they made me."

"They *made* you? *Made* you?"

"Yeah. You know...identified me."

"I know what it means, but this isn't an episode of *NCIS*. This is real life and you have zero training in this type thing."

She smiled. "Well, I do have some training. I mean, I did kick their asses a bit."

"They had guns! They could have shot you dead right there in the street. It was a stupid thing to do. If you want to be a team then you have to display some level of discipline and self-control."

"Like you did a few moments ago as you pistol-whipped a man?"

Touché.

"Bethany, this isn't a game. If you can't promise me right now that you won't do anything like that again, then I'll drive us straight to the police and we'll take our chances with them."

"Point taken," she said. "It was impulsive and I won't do anything like that again."

"Promise me."

"I promise."

"Thank you."

We drove in silence and followed the Buick as they got off the highway and headed up small roads into Pittsburgh's North Hills.

"You must have changed at lot over the years," said Bethany.

"What do you mean?"

"You yelled at me."

"So?"

"So, yelling isn't very Tin Man-like. Maybe stoicism isn't

your thing anymore."

I wasn't sure how to respond. Eventually, I said, "Things are different for me than they used to be. Everything is changing."

"What's different?"

"Now I have something to lose."

She reached over and squeezed my hand. Cujo snarled.

Bethany stroked his head and said, "Now, what makes you think they are taking us to Dennis Hackney?"

"It's logical. We know they aren't local cops and they certainly aren't feds. They aren't part of the drug gang that wants me dead and I don't think they are affiliated with Metal Security. That leaves one party that would be interested in my activities and the photos Nick gave me."

"What could he possibly want from you? You don't have the photos anymore."

"No, but I looked through them and the accompanying notes. Although I wasn't processing information very well at the time, I have a good memory and my thoughts have become clearer. If they researched me, they may know I have a knack for reconstructing scenes in my mind and seeing how things relate to each other."

I was underselling my abilities a bit. Throughout my stints in law enforcement and in the private sector, I'd discovered I possess a level of intuition and analysis most people do not. It's not like I'm psychic, but I'm able to let my eyes go out of focus and, using the information available to me, I become a witness of sorts to the crime. I call these moments my blur-outs. If I'm doped up, they don't happen. I can pull things together when I'm not on my medication, but then the hallucinations pop up and add confusion to my life.

"So, you think Hackney sent these two to your house and one of them took a shot at you?" Bethany asked.

"I don't think the shot Hayes fired into my refrigerator was premeditated. It was a reaction to my attacking her partner. My guess is she has police or military experience and she reacted according to her training."

"So they didn't want to hurt you?"

Bayless and Hayes pulled into a private drive. A man I assumed was a Secret Service agent was standing in front of a large iron gate. Bayless leaned out his window and had a conversation with the agent, likely explaining that Hackney was expecting us.

I shook my head. "I don't think they would mind hurting either one of us. I'm guessing they are officially on Hackney's payroll as security consultants or staff and they are more mercenary than anything else."

"Why would the Secret Service tolerate them being around?"

"They don't have a choice," I replied. "If Hackney says they're his employees and their backgrounds come back relatively clean, then they won't be considered threats. In fact, they won't even get searched for weapons if they've been cleared."

"You're kidding."

"Nope."

"Well, you have their weapons under your seat. I can't imagine they are going to react well to that!"

"We'll see. The level of protection for a candidate is different than it is for the president or vice president. If Hackney tells the agents to let us in unmolested, then that's likely what's going to happen."

"And if it isn't?"

"Then they won't let us in, but I doubt we would be arrested. Probably not."

"Your confidence is astounding."

"The good news is that Secret Service agents are basically cops. Unlike some security forces in the world, they will give warnings and won't shoot unarmed civilians."

"It's not like that everywhere?"

"No," I said. "Obviously there are some third-world countries and dictatorships where rules don't apply. But even the Israeli Shin Bet react differently to threats. I've heard if they are around a protectee and an attack occurs, they'll open fire on anyone standing other than their own people or the protectee. Jackie once told me she worked a joint detail with the Shin Bet and she'd been told that if the Israelis pull out their submachine guns then to hit the ground because pretty much anyone standing up is going to be treated as a threat."

"That's...extreme."

"That's the reality when you're surrounded by people who want to wipe you off the planet."

The agent moved to the speaker box pressed a button and leaned down to say something. The gate opened and the Buick in front of us pulled forward. The agent waved us forward and stared us down as we drove past. I thought we were in the clear, but then two members of the Secret Service's Uniform Division appeared from the sides and signaled for us to stop. One of the officers ran a mirror under the car and another had us pop the trunk. After the explosion at the Museum of Art, the Secret Service was going to at least make sure no large explosives got near the residence. Bethany and I wondered what would happen if they decided to search inside the car and found the pistols. We needn't have worried, as we got waved through.

Bethany said, "I can't believe they didn't search the car."

"Well, I'm sure Bayless and Hayes will make sure we aren't allowed to take the weapons inside. But still, you're right. It does seem strange security isn't tighter around Dennis Hackney after an assassination attempt."

I followed the Buick halfway around a circular driveway. The car stopped in front of the mansion and I left about forty feet between our vehicles. After putting the car in park I cracked the windows for Cujo.

"He'll have to stay in the car," I said as I reached under the seat. Keeping my eyes on Hayes and Bayless, I quickly took turns handling each of the pistols and metallic sounds filled the car.

"What are you doing?" asked Bethany.

"Stealing something," I said, keeping my hands out of view.

I finished what I was doing as Bayless and Hayes approached the car. I pulled both guns up and put them in one hand. With the other I opened the door and got out, but dropped the guns on my seat so as to not alarm any watchful Secret Service agents. Bethany got out on her side and scanned the front of the mansion.

"There are your guns," I said, pointing to them.

Bayless came around to my side of the car and I stood aside. He reached in the car and covertly slid each of the pistols into his waistband. He raised his bruised and bloodied face and his eyes met mine.

"I owe you," he said with malice.

"You owe me a refrigerator."

He turned his head, spat, then said, "Follow me."

We followed the two up to the unlocked front door and Hayes pushed it open. Hayes stepped in and Bayless took a position to our rear.

"Don't touch anything," Hayes commanded.

Once we were all inside, she walked up to Bayless and held out her hand. He reached in his waistband and drew the two pistols I'd returned to him. Both guns were nearly identical, but I'd noticed one had a custom grip with a raised texture. Bayless handed the one with the standard grip to Hayes. She pulled back the slide far enough to check if there was still a round in the chamber. Finding there was and determining the weapon was still loaded, she let the slide return back to its normal position and slid the gun into a holster on her hip. Bayless took her cue, checked his weapon, and then holstered his gun as well.

"Come on," said Hayes as she resumed walking us through the foyer.

Other than our footsteps, the house seemed dead silent. Echoes followed us until we reached a marble staircase that spiraled upward.

Hayes led the way, displaying a slight limp and bracing herself with the railing as she ascended. Bethany and I walked side by side and she tapped me on the arm having noticed Hayes's limp. With pride she whispered, "I did that."

I did my best not to roll my eyes and glanced back at Bayless who was walking fine, but wasn't going to get any modeling jobs in the near future. Hayes hung a right at the top of the stairs and approached a wooden door. She gave it three hard knocks before turning the knob. We entered the room which was something between an office and a library. It wasn't the office where Hackney had been sitting in one of the photos I'd seen. We were surrounded by built-in bookshelves and furniture ten times more expensive than anything I had gone around delivering with Juan. Across the room, behind the biggest oak desk I'd ever seen, sat an imposing figure, but not the one I thought would greet us. However, now I understood why security wasn't quite as tight as one might expect.

"Mr. Galloway and Ms. Nolan. Thank you for coming."

The woman stood and walked around the desk with more grace than most people could display in a lifetime. Her black dress hardly seemed to move as her long legs strode forward. Her toned arms swung with a cool smoothness when she approached and the gentle sway of her movements caused the waves of her brown hair to drift over her high cheekbones. Although I knew her to be close to sixty, she appeared to belong more with Generation X than with the Baby Boomers. She paused, scrutinized her battered employees, and her expression went from welcoming to patronizing.

"I believe I told both of you to be polite to Mr. Galloway. By all accounts, he's a dangerous man—as it seems you have learned." She moved close to Hayes and examined her face more closely. "Although I think hitting women is a little excessive. But then again, you killed a woman once didn't you? So perhaps a few bruises and cuts aren't the end of the world."

"Actually, that was me," said Bethany, raising her hand. Then, she pointed to Bayless and said, "And I did some of the damage to Bayless too."

"Bayless?" said the woman. "Oh, of course. I see."

"Their names aren't Bayless and Hayes?" Bethany asked.

"No," said the woman. "I'm afraid not. However, their names are not important."

"Well, are you going to tell us who you are?" Bethany asked. "Because I've seen Dennis Hackney on television and I'm not seeing the resemblance."

The woman looked at me and seemed to be expecting me to say something, but I remained quiet.

"You don't recognize me?" said the woman. "I'm on the news as well, although I admit I don't run to every camera."

"No," said Bethany. "The news is depressing."

She smiled. "I'm Alana Hackney. Dennis is my husband."

"You sent these two goons after us?" said Bethany.

Alana Hackney grinned and said, "That sounds a bit dramatic."

Bethany said, "Well, they threatened Trevor in his home and then tried to kill him."

Alana waved a hand. "All a big misunderstanding. I had asked my friends here to investigate a certain matter and they approached the job with more enthusiasm than I would have liked. The gunshot was an unfortunate consequence of Mr. Galloway attacking them. I certainly did not intend for any harm to come to Mr. Galloway."

Bethany eyed the woman with skepticism and asked, "What is it you want? Why are we here?"

Alana stared at me again. I waited her out.

"Mr. Galloway, you haven't said a word. Would you like to contribute to this discussion?"

I didn't speak. In fact, I wasn't seeing Alana Hackney. I was only hearing the conversation from a distance and the voices were muffled as if being heard through the floorboards of an old house. The elaborately decorated office morphed into a dingy, nondescript room. Nick Van Metre was tied to a chair, his face bloodied and eyes swollen shut. A silhouette was standing in front of him, yelling something I couldn't understand. He punched Nick in the face repeatedly. He stopped and a large water jug and a towel appeared beside the chair. Another shadowy figure appeared behind Nick and yanked his head back. Suddenly, the towel was over Nick's face and water was being poured into his breathing passages.

Drowning.

Restrained.

Bound to a chair.

He was being waterboarded.

My eyes focused on the wall on the opposite side of the room. A bulletin board hung on flimsy paneling and several items were pinned to the board. Somehow I found myself standing in front of the board and I could see the items were the photos Nick had given to me. Most of the photos were arranged in two rows, with twelve on the top row and eleven on the bottom. Twenty-three photos. I searched the board and the wall for the twenty-fourth picture. My eyes dropped to the floor and I saw something crumpled at my feet. I heard Nick gasp and beg, but I couldn't take my attention off the wadded up paper out of fear it would vanish. I reached down, picked up the item, and unfolded the twenty-fourth photo—the one that didn't belong.

This wasn't how it normally worked. The blur-out was allowing my mind to assume facts that weren't in evidence and my subconscious seemed to be trying to tell me something. This wasn't a real place. It was nowhere I'd been and nowhere I would ever be. It was manufactured and unverified. Still, there was something here.

I spun to say something to Nick, but my throat felt like it had closed up. With one hand, I grabbed at my throat and hurried to where Nick was bound. One of the figures removed the towel and someone leaned Nick forward so he could cough up the fluid. He struggled for every breath and pleaded with his captors. Then his wet face turned up toward me. His hair falling over his face.

"Do you see what's missing?" he kept saying. "Do see the negative space?"

"Trevor?"

Bethany's voice made it through the fog.

"Trevor? Are you okay?"

The rows of books came into focus and I inhaled deeply, having not done so for several seconds.

"Do you need to sit down, Mr. Galloway?" said Alana.

I shook my head and steadied myself.

"In that case, I wanted to ask you for a favor," she said.

"We'll do it," I responded.

Alana glanced at Bethany and then me.

"I haven't asked the question yet."

"We'll take the job."

Bethany put a hand on my shoulder and squeezed. "She isn't asking to hire us for anything."

Alana stood frozen with her mouth open and then said, "Well, actually I am."

"You send people to scare the hell out of him and now you want to hire us?" Bethany asked. "What the hell do you want us to do?"

"She wants us to find the missing photo," I said.

"What missing photo?" Bethany asked. "You threw them away."

I shook my head. "One was switched out. There's one photo in particular she wants and it wasn't in the stack I had. There were twenty-four photos and twenty-three of them were supposedly taken by Chaerea. She wants the one that Nick held back."

"Wait," said Bethany. "First you took a job to find Chaerea and you couldn't do that. Now you want to work for this woman? Have you lost your mind?"

"I found Chaerea," I said, not taking my eyes off Alana.

Bethany held her hands out in exasperation. "When did this happen? Between furniture deliveries? Would you like to tell me who Chaerea is?"

I nodded forward. Alana Hackney clasped her hands in front of her.

"Oh, my. You are everything as advertised, Mr. Galloway. It's going to be a pleasure working with you. Shall we discuss your fee?"

Bethany was incredulous. "Whoa, whoa, whoa. We aren't working for you rich crackpots. Let's go, Trevor." She took a step toward the door.

Alana Hackney grinned and said, "I'll pay you each fifty thousand dollars, plus expenses. Half in advance and half upon recovery."

Bethany did a one-hundred-eighty-degree turn and said, "I can take cash or a check."

FRAME 12

While no longer carrying the amount of muscle that had made him a star lacrosse player at the University of Pennsylvania, Hackney managed to avoid the curse of obesity that plagued so many men his age. Rather than use the fitness center at the Duquesne Club downtown, he preferred to push himself at the less-exclusive Legacy Training Center in Ross Township. He was one of several people using the elliptical machines lined up on one a side of a room. The rest of the space was filled with weight machines sorted by whichever muscle group the mechanism was designed to attack.

Hackney's was in mid-stride, gliding through the low-impact skiing motion forced by the device. His face displayed intensity, but not strain. Strain wouldn't play well with the voters. Intensity he could sell. I couldn't tell how much he might have exerted himself at the point the photo was taken, but he wasn't drenched with perspiration. If any of the other people who were there sculpting their bodies took notice of Hackney, it wasn't obvious. Other than one Metal Security agent standing deep in the background, nobody else in the photo was looking at the man who was starting to make not only local, but national headlines.

Hackney was staring straight ahead. Even though he was frozen in time, there was no question he was striding forward with an unstoppable sense of purpose.

* * *

"All right, Mr. Galloway. How did you know?" Alana asked.

"How did I know what?"

She moved to the front of her desk and sat on top of it, crossing her long legs. "Let's start with how you knew Nick switched out one of the photos."

I started to respond, but Alana interrupted.

"Oh, my. How rude of me. I'm so sorry." She stood and walked over to a cabinet wedged between the built-in bookshelves. She pressed a button and the cabinet opened, revealing a fully stocked bar, complete with an ice box. She immediately began fixing a drink. "Can I get either of you a beverage?"

Bethany took a few steps toward the bar and squinted. Then her eyes got big. "Absinthe? Does that bottle say 'Absinthe'?"

Alana smiled. "Yes. I know it's not common and has a reputation for being on the dangerous side, but it's quite safe if procured from the right source. Would you like to try some?"

Bethany shook her head.

"I'm guessing this isn't on the drink list at Applebee's."

"How do you know I work there?"

Alana didn't answer, but held a drink out for Bethany.

"Here's a rum and Coke. I hope that will suffice."

Bethany tentatively took the drink. "It's my favorite mixed drink. Thank you." Then looking at me she said, "What a coincidence."

"And for you, Mr. Galloway?" asked our hostess.

"I'm fine."

She proceeded to fix her own drink, a martini, while resuming her questioning. "So, how did you come to realize Nick switched out one of the pictures?"

"On the surface, all of the photos seemed to be different," I said. "None of them were taken in the same location. Your husband was never in the same pose. There didn't appear to be any attempt to replicate the angle the photo was snapped from. I've come to realize the key to understanding the photos was to look at the one difference and the one similarity. The difference told me which photo was switched out and the similarity told me you are Chaerea."

"What was the difference?" Alana asked.

"There was one photo, I believe it was the sixth in the pack, in which your husband was sitting in a chair. According to the notes I read, he couldn't recall the location. I don't remember everything about the photo, but I do recall the background was blurry and Mr. Hackney appeared posed."

"So you figured that was the aberration since the locations of the other photos were known?"

I shook my head. "That shot was the only one in which your husband was the only person in the frame. There was no security. No staff. No one else. But, you're partially right. The lack of a solid location and the blurry background did lead me to the conclusion that not only is that photo different from the others in the lack of description, but also in how it was taken. He posed for that one."

Wordlessly, the woman who might be the next first lady took her drink to a plush sofa in the middle of the room. She sat and arranged herself like a feline.

Alana finished a sip of her drink and said, "That's a big leap to make."

I said, "Bold leaps are what you're about to pay us for. That and our silence."

Nobody spoke. I locked eyes with Alana Hackney. Her perpetual smile faded.

Bethany said, "Okay. Maybe she slipped me some absinthe after all. I'm going to need someone to lay all this out for me."

"If you don't mind," I said to Alana, while walking to the bar, "I think I will have that drink."

I examined a twenty-one-year-old bottle of Balvenie scotch. I had no idea how much it cost, but since I didn't know, it must have been a lot. I found a glass and poured generously. It tasted expensive, like I could fall into it and envelop myself in power and clarity. Like drifting into one of my blur-outs.

"People love a good assassination plot," I said. "It generates publicity. It generates a sense of drama. There is a natural tendency to sympathize with the intended target, which is especially valuable to a politician who isn't especially charismatic and champions controversial viewpoints. Early in the campaign, there was an idea. Dennis Hackney would have a stalker. This stalker would seem to have incredible access and be undetectable. Before the Secret Service, along with all of their protective intelligence resources, assumed responsibility for Mr. Hackney's security, the story would leak. The leak would undoubtedly come from an unidentified member of the campaign staff or from someone inside Metal Security, but not until I was fully involved in the case. With my involvement, no press outlet in the country could resist those headlines."

I took another drink from my glass and then realized I should be careful. I'd barely touched the stuff since my release and my tolerance was probably akin to an anorexic gnat.

"Are you saying Nick was part of a scheme?" asked Bethany.

I nodded. "I'm afraid so. The plan was for him to hire me to track down the fictional Chaerea."

"Why you?" she asked.

"It gave the Hackneys maximum flexibility. Down the road, they could claim Chaerea got away because I'm nuts and incompetent. Or, they could turn things around and try to make it look like *I* was Chaerea. After all, I'd be the perfect patsy. They've already demonstrated they are extremely good at covering their tracks."

"But Nick was your friend. Why would he go along with any of this?"

"I have one reason and one theory," I said. "The reason is he wasn't my friend. He acted as if he didn't harbor any ill will about Jackie getting killed, but he blamed me. Even if I wasn't directly responsible, he must have felt as if my involvement in her case led to her death. Regardless, he determined I was an expendable psychopath and *every* good conspiracy story needs one of those.

"So that's your reason. What is your theory," said Alana who had shown no reaction to anything I had said thus far.

"I'll get to that," I promised. Then turning to Bethany, I said, "A few things went wrong with the plan. First, I ended up turning them down. Second, I threw the photos away, but they couldn't be certain I really tossed them out. Third, someone really did try to kill Dennis Hackney in what had to be an inside job. Now we have the perfect storm of a fake conspiracy meeting a real conspiracy; everyone has secrets they want kept, and the only thing I know for sure is who killed Nick Van Metre."

"Who?" asked Bethany.

"I've already called the police," I lied. "They'll be here shortly and I'll discuss it with them."

"I hope your theory wasn't that I had something to do with Nick's murder," said Alana, still keeping a poker face.

"It isn't."

"Then what is your theory?"

"You were able to get Nick to join in on this plan because the two of you were sleeping together."

That got a reaction.

She stood up, stormed over to me, and threw her drink in my face. Fortunately, she had been giving the martini as much attention as she had my explanation and only a few drops flew out. However, an olive did hit me in the forehead.

"How dare you. I'm insulted you would accuse me of such a thing," she shouted.

I used the back of my sleeve to wipe my face and head. "No you aren't. And there's no need for all of that. If you open the door, you'll see your henchmen are gone. They would have hit the road the second they heard me say I'd figured out who killed Nick and had called the police."

"What? They work for me. They wouldn't have hurt Nick."

"Call for them," I suggested.

She placed the martini glass down on a table, walked to the

door and opened it. Not finding them posted in the hallway, she yelled their names, which were apparently Tyler and Kay. Tyler and Kay weren't responding and I knew they weren't going to respond.

Alana came back into the room looking shell-shocked. "They've worked for me for two years. They were on my husband's staff before coming to me."

"They're essentially mercenaries," I said. "You were outbid by someone."

"By who?"

I didn't answer.

"It's all about the photo, isn't it?" said Bethany. "Tell us about the missing photo. Hell, tell us all about everything."

Alana went to the sofa and this time there was no grace in the way she fell into it. "You're right. Except Nick and I weren't just sleeping together. We loved each other very much. It's not what you think, we weren't going behind Dennis's back or anything. Dennis knew about us and he couldn't have cared less. In fact, he was glad Nick was onboard with the plan. In hindsight, the entire enterprise was amateurish and dangerous. But we worried Dennis's views wouldn't be enough to carry the popular vote. He was going to need every bit of reality-TV drama out there to pull this off. So, we decided to start early with the Chaerea plan. However, it never really got off the ground because you turned down the case and got rid of the photos."

"Nick said he still had the originals," I said.

"They were stolen from his home," said Alana.

"And Nick switched the one picture out of the pack before he gave it to me," I said. "Why?"

"I can't tell you," she said.

"Then we walk," said Bethany.

Alana looked at me for help, but none was forthcoming. "You heard her. Full disclosure or we walk away and watch as everything crashes down around you and your husband for employing two murderers."

"Three," Bethany said. "Indirectly."

I looked at her questioningly. She gave a slight shrug and pointed awkwardly in my direction.

"Three," I corrected.

Alana closed her eyes and tilted her head back. In that position, her age showed through the veins in her neck. Slowly, she lowered her head and opened her eyes.

She asked, "Do you know the name Joseph Obol?"

FRAME 13

There is nothing flashy about the Brentwood VFW post off Saw Mill Run Boulevard. The American flag flies near the street. There are no sizable windows on any side of the building. Depending on the direction one faces, the parking lot is a stone's throw away from a Dollar Store, a grocery store, or a car wash. The structures aren't particularly modern—mostly compilations of yellow and white painted brick and occasionally some sheet metal. Truth be told, if you removed the vehicle models and the image of Dennis Hackney entering his limousine after giving a short speech, the photo could have been taken anytime between 1995 and present day. His security is there. Some of his staff is heading to vehicles. I see Nick. It's the first time he's appeared in a photo. His presence makes me cognizant of an absence.

Scrutinizing photographs can be like examining any type of image, be it an elaborate painting or complex drawing. It can even be easy to lose yourself in the beautiful business of a well-designed tattoo. I once knew this tattoo artist who operated off of East Carson Street. She did amazing work and people waited for months to get an appointment. She was great with all styles, but her best work was when she created an image by using the negative space. She'd design incredible tattoos by leaving areas of untouched skin and then coloring designs around the unshaded areas. Sometimes it's what's missing that completes the picture.

* * *

"It's a name I can't forget," Alana said while downing her second martini. "However, I didn't know his face and it seems my ignorance has created complications."

We were all seated now. Bethany and I dangled our empty glasses over the arms of our chairs while Alana spoke.

"Nick didn't recognize the name and when we realized we had a photo of my husband speaking to Joseph Obol...well, we knew it had to disappear. Unfortunately, Nick didn't exactly follow through."

Bethany asked, "Who is Joseph Obol?"

"He's a Ugandan war criminal, my dear. My husband was photographed with the man responsible for the deaths of fifty-four villagers who had refused to join his doomed rebellion. There is an image of Dennis and Obol together, laughing and smiling. Can you imagine any worse imagery? Even my smooth-talking husband wouldn't be able to manage that level of fall-out."

Bethany asked, "How does your husband know Mr. Obol?"

"It's complicated," Alana replied.

"No. *He's* complicated," Bethany said, nodding to me. "This simply requires some clarification."

Alana took in a deep breath and said, "Dennis is an extremely intelligent man. He has made his fortune by reading the tea leaves and correctly predicting which stocks to buy, which contributions to make, and who to get in his pocket. Uganda is a nation rich in resources like oil and gold and a few years ago my dear husband decided the political winds of change were blowing in that hellhole. So, he backed their most dominant liberation movement, or resistance army, or whatever you want to call it. Dennis was so confident he was backing the right horse, he allowed himself to get close to their leader, Joseph Obol. They met in Uganda and Kenya. They wined and dined. Well, Dennis doesn't drink, so there wouldn't have been wine, but I'm sure they shared prostitutes and all the usual things that happened in my husband's depraved world back in those days. Anyway, while my husband's initial intent was to earn Obol's trust, the two of them ended up becoming friends. Needless to say, this was many years ago and the rebellion ended badly. Obol became a fugitive and Dennis pretended the two of them had never been anything but passing acquaintances who had mutual friends in the business world. Since then, my husband has been careful to never mention Obol's name or make anyone feel the need to look into his Ugandan dealings."

Bethany leaned forward and asked, "When was the photo of Obol and your husband taken?"

"Two weeks before Nick approached Mr. Galloway."

Bethany was stunned. "Wait. Was this missing photo taken in the US?"

Alana nodded. "We took a quick trip down to Savannah, Georgia where Dennis is on the board of a large lumber company. While he was there, he decided to visit an African relief organization called Famine Assist that operates out of a warehouse that used to be a helicopter hangar. Now, Dennis doesn't give a damn about hungry kids in African countries, but he knows a good photo op when he sees one. He arranged to head down to the port, visit the warehouse, and meet some of the organization's representatives. Dennis was doing his thing, shaking hands, smiling at and complimenting everyone he met, and then I noticed he froze when he saw a black man with eyeglasses standing away from the crowd in a dark corner. The man was watching Dennis and seemed content with staying in the shadows. Dennis tried not to show a reaction, but I could tell something had him rattled.

"Then, after Dennis mingled with the employees and volunteers an appropriate amount of time and people had become distracted by their own little conversations, he wandered over to the man in the corner. I was surprised when the two of them embraced. They spoke quietly and I couldn't hear what they were discussing, but it was obvious they were thrilled to see each other. Later, Dennis told me Obol had managed to falsify his identity and get on with an aid organization. The degenerate sociopath has been living on the Georgia coast for years under the name Ben Hershey, and nobody has had a clue."

"Let me make sure I understand this," said Bethany. "Did you take all the photos?"

Alana finished her drink and wagged a finger. "You're being quiet again, Mr. Galloway. I'm not one to get nervous, but you make me nervous when you're quiet. Why don't you answer that one?" She waved her glass in the air as if playing to a crowd. "You're the *answer man.*"

"You took some of them."

"And how did you know?" Alana asked.

"Because the similarity in all the photos was that you weren't in them. My guess is several of them were taken by your two goons, Tyler and…"

"Kay," Bethany had to remind me. Yep, one scotch was enough.

"Right. Kay. Because there would be times too many eyes were on you. There were also some shots of your husband getting in or out of limos. Assuming you rode with him, someone would have had to have set up ahead of time or stayed behind. That rules you out, unless you arrived or departed separate from your husband, which was probably rare."

Alana stood, paced, unsteady on her feet. "It was stupid not to include me in any of the pictures."

"Nick, Tyler, and Kay probably didn't realize they were doing it," I said. "Your exclusion led me to believe someone wanted to distance you from the potential exposure as much as possible. It may not even have been conscious."

Alana shook her head. "Foolish."

Her gaze dropped to the floor. Sincerity, laced with inebriation. She swallowed hard and pulled herself back.

"Tyler, Kay, and Nick were with us on the trip to Savannah.

Tyler snapped the photo of Dennis with Obol. He didn't know of its significance at the time."

"But you had to have known Nick might include that photo in the packet he gave to Trevor." Bethany said. "Why wouldn't you destroy the photo?"

"I didn't know about it at the time," said Alana. "I'm sure it should have occurred to me that a photo from the Savannah stop might be included, but the truth is we attend so many events, I tend to lose track. I had no idea the hired help had managed to get a photo of my husband conversing with a bloodthirsty killer."

Alana tapped a fingernail against her glass while walking to a window. Nobody spoke for several seconds as she looked out onto her property.

"I wish we would have never contrived this scheme. The photos. Chaerea. If things weren't already spinning out of control, then someone tried to assassinate my husband with a bomb. Who would do such a thing?"

I had theories and the strongest one started with the two mercenaries that had just bolted from the mansion. Tyler and Kay not jumping to the top of her suspect list told me something about Alana's mindset. She wasn't someone who easily accepted the fact she could be misled. She'd been deceived and likely outbid. I wondered which bothered her more. Regardless, I didn't respond to her question.

Keeping her back turned to us, Alana spoke. Professional. Dignified. Defiant. "Dennis is in Harrisburg today and returns tomorrow. Shall I tell him I've retained your services and that you will be retrieving the photograph in question?"

"Why didn't Nick give me the Obol photo?" I asked. "Why switch that one out and not tell you? You said Nick didn't understand the importance of the photo, but he must have realized it at some point."

Our hostess turned our direction, but kept her eyes lowered. "Before meeting with you, Nick overheard my husband speaking to an associate about the trip to Savannah. The name Joseph Obol was mentioned and Nick, who was knowledgeable about international affairs, put two and two together. Nick removed the photo and plugged in a posed publicity shot that was never used. I found this out after the fact—after Tyler and Kay visited you. In the days prior to that, Nick and I were not on good terms. We had been arguing quite a bit. I had wanted him to destroy the photo, but he had thought it best to hold on to it in the event..."

"In the event he might want to use it against your husband," Bethany said.

"I'm afraid so," said Alana. "While I cared deeply for Nick, Dennis is my husband and I wouldn't dream of hurting him. Sadly, something had changed in Nick. I asked him if he had given you a copy of the photo, but he refused to give me any details. If it makes any difference, I do apologize for Tyler and Kay's behavior toward you."

"Nick was tortured," I said. "If he had the photograph, he probably gave it up. This may all be an exercise in futility."

Alana wiped a tear away and acted as if I'd never spoken by repeating her previous question. "Shall I tell my husband you will find the photograph?"

I didn't answer her, but asked, "Other than him, you, Tyler, and Kay, who else knows about the photo?"

Alana paused and then said, "I don't know. Now that it's clear I should not have trusted Tyler and Kay, I can't be certain of anything."

"Is it possible Joseph Obol knows?" asked Bethany.

Alana said, "You said I may have been outbid. If Tyler and Kay realized there was money to be made, then perhaps they approached Obol and made a deal with him. I really don't know. Will you help us?"

Bethany glanced over to me, started to speak, but stopped and nodded.

"Yes," I said. "But, we may need something additional on

the back end."

"Money isn't a problem, Mr. Galloway. It doesn't grow on trees, but political donations do."

"It's not money," I said. "We have some people in law enforcement looking at us, or at least me, pretty closely. It's possible your husband may need to use his influence to ensure valuable agency resources aren't being wasted investigating the wrong people. Namely, me."

Alana turned toward us. "Why would anyone be looking at you?"

"The Pittsburgh Police Department thinks I might have killed Nick."

"Why would you kill Nick?"

"I wouldn't have," I said. "And the Secret Service and FBI are wondering if I didn't try to blow up your husband."

"For what possible reason?"

I shrugged and said, "I don't meet the state's strictest definition of 'sane.'"

"Fine. Is there anyone else you've managed to aggravate?"

"There is a slight possibility a drug gang is still hoping to execute me, but that's a long shot."

Alana sighed. "Does this gang have a name?"

I hesitated. "The EEDC."

"Is ABBA also on your trail? Perhaps hoping to make you a dancing queen?"

Bethany stifled a laugh. Then, I heard an exasperated sigh come from the corner of the room. Lukas Derela, apparently unhappy about the label being affixed to his aforementioned gang, was standing with his arms crossed, a sneer on his face.

"Idiot," he hissed. "We need a divorce attorney, not a job."

The comment gave me pause. It wasn't like Derela to make jokes, but I guess he'd had enough of me. I'd certainly had enough of his dead ass. Well, I decided if the acronym pissed off my worst hallucination, then I was sticking with EEDC.

"That's it," I said to Alana. "We may need you and your

husband to run some interference when we wrap this up. But, we'll take the job."

Alana raised her eyebrows. "I admit, I thought you would have some reservations. Although the allure of money is powerful, you've now had time to process the facts and I'm sure you've had time to formulate the most important question of all."

"You mean the question of whether you had Nick killed?" Bethany asked.

"Precisely."

"You didn't," Bethany replied.

"What makes you so sure?"

Bethany looked to me and then back to our hostess. "Because if you did, Trevor would know. And I have a feeling you're smart enough that if you had anything to do with killing Nick, you never would have let Trevor get into the same room with you."

"I think I'll pay you in cash," said Alana. "No need to leave a paper trail and raise any bothersome questions."

"Of course," I said.

"I will ask that you check in with me every couple of days. Unlike my husband, I'm not a micromanager, but I do wish to be updated on your progress."

"Of course."

"Do you need me to get my driver to take you anywhere?"

"We brought a car," said Bethany.

Alana walked to her desk, retrieved a pen and paper, and handed them to me.

"I'll go get your first payment. While I'm doing that, would you mind writing down how I can reach you?"

Alana left the room and I wrote down our phone numbers.

Bethany said, "Are we really doing this?"

"If you want to. You can still walk away."

She gave the pretense of thinking it over before saying, "In for a dime, in for fifty thousand dollars."

"I'm pretty sure that's not the expression."

I finished writing down our information and placed the pad and pen on the desk.

I said, "We'll have to take time off from work. We're leaving town."

"For fifty grand, I think I just quit Applebee's. Wait...where are we going?"

"We have a new variable to explore."

"Joseph Obol," she said.

"Ever been to Savannah?" I asked.

"No."

"It's beautiful. Historic architecture. Horse-drawn carriages, trees filled with Spanish moss—"

"Ugandan warlords...let's do it! Are we flying or driving?"

That was a tough one. The potential of being on an airplane with a chatterbox hallucination in a nearby seat wasn't particularly appealing. The thought of going on a long car trip with an extra passenger of my own mental manufacturing was no more pleasant. Oh, well. Better to rip it off like a bandage.

"Let's fly. I just have to mail a package first."

Bethany smiled and said, "Take a trip down south on someone else's dime. Get away from some badges who have it out for you. See if we can find a photo that's probably lost anyway. And if we can't find it, then maybe the political fortunes of some rich, right-wing wahoo get knocked back into the Confederacy. I mean, think about it—if that's the worst that can happen, this trip is going to rock."

FRAME 14

The organizers for the one-hundred-twenty-five-year celebration of the Phipps Conservatory and Botanical Gardens spared no expense. Tall cocktail tables had been lined up in neat rows throughout the Special Events Hall and men in tuxedos stood aside women in glittering gowns. The photo was taken from an elevated position and from far enough away to capture most of the room. It takes a second to locate Hackney. He's in the bottom right of the photo, standing at one of the tables, speaking with three individuals—all men. Metal Security was easy to spot since they were in suits, not tuxes, and were the only ones other than the wait staff and Hackney not downing drinks. Nick's in the top right of the photo. He's standing post, as they say in that line of work. There are two other Metal Security officials in the room, each located far enough away to give the protectee some privacy, but close enough to react.

The event appears to be calm. Subdued. I reexamine the photograph from left to right. Top to bottom. When I get midway down and to the right, my eyes dart back to the left. There is a man with his hands in his pockets standing at a table in the center of the room. I don't know why I've keyed in on him and although I can see only the top of his head there is something about his shape, his form that draws me in. At some point, I'll have to go back through the photos because I get the sense I've seen him before. It's there, but it won't stick and I can't tell if my haywire brain is trying to tell me this is relevant.

* * *

Savannah
Two Days Later

The man behind the counter said something. *Focus.*

"Hey! Are you okay, mister?"

The sound of sirens rushing by on the street. Smoke in my nostrils. The blast of a fire truck air horn. Then another.

A convenience store. I was in a convenience store.

"Are you hurt? Do you want me to try to flag down one of those fire trucks or police cars?"

I looked back toward the glass doors that led to the street and squinted as more spinning red lights cut through the night. When there was a lull between the beams, I caught my reflection in the storefront glass. I was covered in soot and blood.

"Dude. Were you near the river? I felt that explosion in my chest; you know what I'm sayin'? It knocked some of the shit in here off the shelves."

The warehouse. Yeah. I was in the warehouse. I was in the fucking warehouse.

I pulled my cell phone out of my pocket and stared at the cracked screen. When I powered on my phone, it appeared as if I had about a dozen missed calls and voice mails from Chase and several others from blocked numbers. I'd call Chase. No need to call Bethany. No need.

"So, are you calling an ambulance or what? It's not like we do much business, but I don't want you scaring away—"

I glared at the man and his hands flew up as he struck a robbery victim pose. His name tag read *Manny* and his face read passive. Passive wasn't going to be a problem. I could deal with him.

I called Chase, who picked up immediately.

"Where the hell are you?"

"Savannah."

"When did you get there?"

"What?" My ears were ringing. My body felt concussed.

"When did you arrive?" he asked.

"A couple of days ago," I said. "Listen—"

"No, you listen," Chase barked. "When *exactly* did you leave Pittsburgh?"

I wasn't sure why this was important, but I wasn't going to get anywhere with Chase until I pacified him.

"We left Wednesday morning. Our flight boarded at seven."

"So Bethany is with you?"

"She came here with me," I said weakly.

"Alana Hackney was beaten to death on Tuesday night. The Secret Service logged two unidentified, but escorted guests in earlier in the afternoon. Those guests departed and nobody heard from Mrs. Hackney for quite some time. Eventually, she was discovered bludgeoned in her office. She'd left a safe open in her bedroom and there was a receipt in her handwriting indicating she was planning on paying you a large amount of cash. Your names and phone numbers were on a paper at the scene. When word got out that Alana Hackney had been murdered, all hell broke loose and our guys and the FBI joined the party. The next thing I know, there's a big powwow going on in the foyer with all your old friends: Ross from the FBI, Kasper from the Secret Service, and Langdale and Gerchak from Pittsburgh PD. One of them starts showing your photos to the agent who had been working the gate and *voila*. You and Bethany are currently wanted for questioning in the murder of Mrs. Alana Hackney. There's a BOLO out for you now and I'm sure your credit cards and cell phones will be tracked shortly."

More sirens and air horns screamed from the street and then retreated into the distance.

Chase continued, "Now, I know you didn't kill her. But there are people here who need to talk to you. I'm also hearing that there a YouTube video floating around of a woman who looks an awful lot like Bethany beating the hell out of two members of Dennis Hackney's staff."

"Alana's staff," I corrected, although I should have kept my mouth shut.

"Jesus. *His* staff. *Her* staff. It's all the same. If you combine this with the whole Chaerea thing, Nick's murder, and you saying that police impersonators shot at you in your house, and your record, these aren't the best of times. Truth be told, I'd say you and Bethany are currently the most wanted people in America."

I walked over to the refrigerator section of the store, grabbed a cold bottle of water off one of the shelves, and chugged half. Manny eyed my every move, but didn't dial 9-1-1. Sirens blared from the street again. I didn't know how many fire stations were in Savannah, but they were all responding.

Chase asked, "What's all that noise? Are you outside a hospital? Is Bethany all right?"

"We were following up on a lead down here. It led us to a warehouse at the port."

"Yeah...and?"

"Things got messy. Then they got rough."

"How rough?" Chase asked tentatively.

"Five or six guys in the warehouse. They hurt Bethany."

"What? Where? What warehouse? I'll send Savannah PD in there now!"

I turned away from Manny and walked to the back of the store. "They can't go there," I said. "It's gone."

Chase breathed slowly into the phone. I knew he was afraid to ask.

"Trevor. What did you do?"

"They hurt her, Chase."

"Trevor."

I spoke slowly. "They...hurt...Bethany."

We didn't speak for half a minute. Finally Chase wasted some words.

"Where are you? I'll find someone I can trust down there and have you picked up. We'll sort this out."

He probably said something else, but I ended the call and headed toward the door. I stopped by the cash register and reached back to get my wallet.

Manny took a step back and said, "Are you robbing me, or what? I know the normal drill, but you don't seem to be on script."

I snagged a one-hundred-dollar bill—one Alana had given me—and put it on the counter.

"For the water and the trouble."

A grin appeared on his face. "Shit, man. Ain't no trouble."

"Are the cameras in here working? Are they recording?"

The grin vanished. I put another hundred on the counter.

"It seems the explosion down the street caused us to have some—what do you call it? Technical difficulties. I do believe those recordings got themselves erased."

"How about your recollection?" I asked.

Manny scratched his head. "Well, you see. I suffer from what you call that Post Stessmatic Syndrome stuff. So when I heard that big boom, I had all sorts of flashbacks." He reached up and slid the bills off the counter and put them in his jeans pocket. "I don't remember much after that."

Manny could have been thirty, but he could have been forty. Either way, I didn't take him for the military type. Whatever flashbacks he had must have been from playing *Call of Duty* on a PlayStation.

I left the store and walked down West Bay Street until I found a Ford pickup truck with South Carolina plates parked in a lot that charged by the hour. The personalized plates read TONYA L. I tossed my cell phone in the bed and decided to let the feds track TONYA L for a while.

The air smelled of smoke and although the pedestrians seemed to notice the commotion going on in the industrial area less than a mile away, there were bars to visit and tours to take. Dozens of people carrying drinks in red plastic Solo cups were actually taking their drinks *toward* the fire to watch the first responders do their work. Savannah buzzed with evening excitement and paid no mind to my disheveled condition. I made a right on Bull Street and walked until I reached Madison Square. I wandered to an unoccupied bench and sat. I needed to think.

We hadn't rushed into things once we'd arrived in town. Bethany and I had checked into a hotel a few blocks away from Forsyth Park and strolled through the tree-lined streets. It had been years since I'd visited the city, but I remembered enough to get us to Monterey Square and the infamous Mercer Williams House. Bethany wasn't familiar with the murder made famous by the book *Midnight in the Garden of Good and Evil*, so I gave her a quick rundown but quickly got bogged down in trying to remember the real facts of the case from the fictionalized account in the book from the completely reconstructed story retold in the movie version. Bethany was patient and listened to both me and occasionally eavesdropped on passing tour guides leading groups around town.

We had lunch at a diner made semi-famous by *Forrest Gump* and plotted our strategy for approaching Joseph Obol, a.k.a. Ben Hershey.

"We have Alana's description, but that's about it," Bethany had said as she poked at a side order of grits she regretted ordering.

We had been at Bethany's apartment on Tuesday night, while someone was killing Alana Hackney. While Bethany packed, I'd gone online and been unsuccessful at finding a home address for Ben Hershey. However, I had no problem finding the website for Famine Assist. While Hershey was listed as an employee, we weren't lucky enough to find an accompanying photo. The pictures that did exist of him online were dated, and I doubted he resembled the warrior with the sharp machete stare who appeared in countless articles related to war crimes.

"Right," I said, watching the foot traffic outside the large glass windows. Savannah's federal courthouse seemed busy and lawyers were bustling up and down stone steps.

"And a stakeout is no good," I added.

Once I'd given up on finding recent photos of Joseph Obol/Ben Hershey, I located the Famine Assist warehouse on Google Maps and called up the satellite view. While it didn't appear the warehouse was part of a secured industrial park, it wasn't a place people could sit in a car and go unnoticed. Much of the structure was surrounded by vast swaths of empty pavement. The exception was the southwest corner of the building, which edged up to a pitiful stretch of grass ending at what appeared to be a thin fence. On the other side of the fence—not more than twenty yards away—sat an oil tank farm, presumably part of another company's facility.

"We could pose as journalists or bloggers doing a story on relief efforts?" Bethany had suggested. "If we get inside, there's a decent chance we'll spot him."

I thought about this while drinking sweet tea—something not easily obtained in Pittsburgh restaurants.

"As unlikely as it is, there is still an element of risk," I said. "If Alana Hackney's hired guns, Tyler and Kay, had been lured away by Ben Hershey, then it's possible he knows our faces."

"So what?" she said. "We're holding all the cards. Let's say he recognizes us. It's an operational warehouse in the middle of the day, with people milling around. All we have to do is confront him and threaten to reveal his real identity if he doesn't tell us what happened to the photo of him and Dennis Hackney. We should be able to tell from his reaction if he had something to do with Nick's murder and knows anything about the missing photo."

She was right. Later, as I sat on the bench, the smell of smoke seeping from my clothing, I understood she was wrong. But at the time, I thought she was right.

"I'm going to have a cool fake reporter name," Bethany decided. "What's the blogger equivalent of Lois Lane?"

"Lois Blane?"

"Good enough."

She smiled.

Then, I felt it. I felt myself smile.

Behind the bench in my darkened corner of Madison Square, I detected movement. I began to turn, but stopped myself.

Knowing I couldn't have been followed, I said, "What do you want, Lukas?"

The response came, but it wasn't from my nemesis of a hallucination. It wasn't any of my hallucinations.

"That's the thing about Savannah," said the voice in a Southern drawl so thick and heavy, any syllable could have cracked one of the bricks under my feet. "It's a wonderful place to hang out, but a *lousy* place to hide out."

Now I *did* turn and take in the form that was mostly shadows and angles. It was too warm for the suede jacket he was wearing and his hands never left the pockets as he revolved around the bench to stand in front of me. The shapes and angles combined with his movements to create something familiar in my mind.

Something must have registered in my eyes, because he said, "You know me."

My eyes dropped to the brick sidewalk and my vision blurred. The sounds of Savannah became muted and the scent of destruction faded from my nostrils. The curtain of the present was pulled up as one with no defined sense of time and space descended.

In the room I'd stood before, or one similar to it, the mental bulletin board filled with rows of photos appeared on the wall in front of me and I studied each image. I stopped at the third frame, and saw Hackney in conversation at the Duquesne Club with the unknown man whose face was not clearly visible, a dark ring around one of the man's fingers. I traced a path along the rows of photos until I reached the ninth frame, where I found

Hackney sitting behind his mansion while an unidentifiable figure wandered away from the landscaped maze. My eyes moved to the fourteenth frame, where Dennis Hackney mingled at the Phipps Conservatory and a solitary figure stood, hands in his pockets, at a cocktail table in the center of the event.

The bulletin board disappeared and my attention returned to the here and now; the real and looming. It had all been a lie. The lie was sold to Nick, who rented it to me, and I gave it away to the world free of charge. Alana Hackney had known exactly what had been in the packet of photos, but she didn't give a damn about an African warlord in hiding. I should have known. Lukas Derela had tried to tell me when he said we needed a divorce attorney instead of a job. I hadn't been pulled into a con job created to generate publicity for an aspiring politician. This wasn't a political operation at all.

It was a goddamned domestic dispute.

The man spoke again. "Well, Mr. Tin Man, I know you." He made a slight gesture with the hand in his right pocket. "We prefer to handle things in a civilized manner down here, but we do what we have to do when necessary. How 'bout you stand up real slow and we go somewhere where we can talk and see if we can't work some things out?"

He took a step forward as he spoke and I could see although we were close in age, he was everything I was not. He was short and stocky and his facial expressions, genuine or not, changed like kaleidoscope patterns. His eyes were bright and spoke their own language and a dimple punctuated his chin. He could have been a soldier of fortune or a lawyer. I knew he was something of both. I also knew there was no way I was going to go with him, unless he said the magic words. Of course, there was no way I was going to tell him what they were. I sat motionless and stared at him. A rare breeze made the Spanish moss sway around us.

"Come on now. I assume you *do* care a little something about that girl you were with."

Those were the magic words.

FRAME 15

The offices of G.B. Barnes Investments are located in the third of six buildings making up PPG Place in downtown Pittsburgh. The structures surround a plaza, creating a set of modern glass castles that, on sunny days, put a blinding accent on the skyline. Dennis Hackney is sitting at one end of a long conference room table of the investment bank, which is one of his many business interests. Seated at the table are eight men and four women. The notes from Metal Security let me know these people are the board of G.B. Barnes Investments, a firm specializing in global investments, particularly in the Middle East, India, and Africa. One of the men appears to be Hispanic and everyone else in the room is Caucasian. The Hispanic man is pointing a finger in Hackney's direction, as if in the middle of an explanation.

Hackney is leaning back in the chair. Comfortable. In command. When Nick first talked to me about the photographs, he'd mentioned the investment bank was a "powder keg," but then there was no further mention of the company. Nick had also mentioned that Hackney was taking heat in the press for not having a single non-white board member ever since a Hispanic male named Hector Solis had been killed in a hit-and-run. Was this photo intended to be a reminder of the cloud hanging over Hackney's head?

"Mine is the silver Volvo. I won't draw attention our way by patting you down, but please do me the courtesy of not making any sudden movements. I wouldn't want to overreact."

With his left hand, he pressed a button on a key fob; lights flashed and doors unlocked. Keeping his right hand in his jacket pocket, he handed me the key.

"You can drive. But please be careful. Pedestrians *always* have the right of way in our little town, or at least they think they do." He smiled.

I walked out into the street and opened the driver's side door. We both slid into our seats simultaneously. As smoothly as he'd gotten into the car, the man withdrew the Smith & Wesson revolver from his jacket pocket, squashing the miniscule hopes I had he'd been bluffing. He wore a black ring on one of the fingers of his right hand. It was a broad textured band. Titanium, I guessed. While managing to keep the gun pointed at me, he buckled his seatbelt and then stared at me.

"Please buckle up. Savannah is a hard-drinking town and unfortunately some of our visitors haven't figured out the best tools for both finding and leaving a good time come with good soles and laces."

I buckled my seatbelt and put my hands on the wheel. The car was in immaculate condition, but I noticed the steering wheel had a gash in it at the two o'clock position. He told me to pull out and head south on Bull Street, so I did.

"I heard you were the quiet type," he said as I crawled along streets meant for horses rather than Swedish luxury cars. "Aren't you going to ask where we're going?"

"What do I call you?" I asked.

"Oh, names, names, names. They are funny things, aren't they?" He nodded forward. "Would you mind making a right when we get to Monterey Square?"

I stopped the car as a gaggle of college kids stumbled across Bull Street, oblivious to all but themselves. One of them, a lanky girl with a blue streak in her hair, clapped her hands softly with each step.

"People are given a name and told they need to make it mean something. They aspire to assign meaning to a series of letters strung together and chosen by someone because of sentiment or tradition. We kneel down and look our children in the eyes and tell them, 'Go out there and make a name for yourself.' But isn't that so incredibly limiting? Why one name? Why not five? Ten?"

I didn't speak. I simply pressed the gas pedal as the street cleared. Monterey Square approached.

"For the sake of simplicity, you can call me Mr. Simon. Now, aren't you going to ask me where we are going?"

"No."

He chuckled and leaned back against the passenger side door.

"My, you are a curious man. By that I mean I find you to be a curiosity, but you certainly do not seem to be inquisitive. I supposed there is irony in that."

He waited for me to talk. I didn't.

"I wasn't sure it would ever happen, but part of me was hoping to have the chance to meet you. So, why aren't you going to ask me where we are headed?"

"Because it doesn't matter."

"And why not?"

"Because Bethany isn't there. And you wouldn't risk telling me her location because I might chance killing or maiming you and going there by myself. I'm not dead on a park bench right now, so you must want something from me. So, our destination is irrelevant. It's the outcome that's important."

Out of the corner of my eye, I could see Mr. Simon nodding in appreciation.

"Turn right here and then left on Whitaker," he told me. Then he added, "I assume you do have *some* questions for me."

I shrugged and this amused him.

"Really? So you do have a basic understanding of who I am."

"I know *what* you are," I replied as I turned left on Whitaker Street. We were flowing away from the bar crowds and becoming submerged in homes that swam in old money. "You're Dennis

Hackney's fixer. You're the guy who takes care of his dirty laundry and creates some for anyone who gets in his way. Hackney has to keep his affiliation with you a secret because of your past. My guess is you're wanted in multiple jurisdictions under several aliases and he probably first linked up with you in Africa around the time he met Joseph Obol. Now, at some point keeping you around at all had to become a calculated risk. When one is talking about the presidency, nobody has a skill set that outweighs the political liability of having a criminal on the payroll. So it's probable you have enough dirt on Hackney that he feels more comfortable keeping you around as an ally rather than paying you off and cutting you loose."

Mr. Simon was quiet for a moment, which seemed to be uncharacteristic for him, so I glanced over. He was less amused than before.

"Make a right down this small street."

He had me cross over to Barnard Street, make another right, and pull up in front of an unassuming two-story brick office building.

"We're going in there to talk," he said as he unfastened his seatbelt and reached across his body for his door handle. "I have an office on the second floor. Actually I own the building, but I only use one office."

I knew if I went inside under these circumstances I was never coming out. I needed to stay in the car a few more minutes.

"Obol is dead," I said.

Mr. Simon's hand dropped from the handle. "I figured as much."

"Nick Van Metre is dead. Alana Hackney is dead. You're on borrowed time. All loose ends have to go. Even you."

A corner of the man's mouth rose. "I'm a resourceful soul, Mr. Galloway, and I have no illusions as to my mortality and expendability. Confidence and competence are useless in the hands of the arrogant. If anything were to happen to me, damaging information would find its way to the right people. My continued well-being is in Mr. Hackney's best interest."

"You're a survivor," I observed. "And you help others survive if it suits you. That's why Joseph Obol settled here in Savannah. You arranged it, but never told Dennis Hackney the details so he was genuinely shocked when he ran into Obol here."

"Mr. Hackney asked me if I could assist Mr. Obol, but didn't want to know specifics. I made the necessary arrangements. Years later, I helped facilitate a meeting between Mr. Hackney and the CEO of a lumber company, which led to him being named to the board of that company, which resulted in Hackney paying a visit to our city not long ago." Mr. Simon slapped his knee as if telling a humorous story to boy scouts around a campfire. "Not in a million years would I have imagined Mr. Hackney would have taken a side trip to the warehouse where I had placed Obol as a staff member." He said the next three words philosophically. "Life. Is. Remarkable."

Mr. Simon pondered this for a few moments and then returned mentally to our still-running Volvo on Barnard Street. I had put the car in park, but periodically pressed the brake pedal.

Finally, he said, "Speaking of which—I do want to hear what happened at that warehouse."

I subtly checked the mirrors. Needing a few more minutes, I told him *exactly* what happened at the warehouse.

Even if Bethany and I had known what Obol looked like, there were too many possible exits to cover from the warehouse complex, so it wouldn't have been possible for us to sit outside a gate and tail him. No, we were going to have to go in there and quietly confront the man without raising any alarms among his peace-loving, humanitarian colleagues. We hoped that if we handled this diplomatically, Obol would have to appreciate our tact.

We would pose as freelance journalists wanting to do a piece for an online magazine that we were starting up. The start-up portion was key, because we didn't have credentials that could survive any kind of online background check. It was a weak cover-story, but all we needed was to get face-to-face with the man they knew as Ben Hershey. The story we were supposedly working on was going to focus on nonprofit organizations delivering foreign aid. As we explained this to the receptionist, we would happen to mention how incredibly insightful it would be if Famine Assist had any employees who had lived in Africa and could lend their perspective to the story.

The ruse worked, to an extent. However, in our minds we had imagined the receptionist at the warehouse office as a middle-aged woman who would greet us with a smile. Or perhaps a surprised face, since she likely didn't receive too many unexpected visitors. She might have pictures of her children on a shelf behind her and probably a calendar on the wall that came free in the mail from a local real estate company.

We were not prepared for the gruff man with the goatee whose neck tattoo was partially obscured by his too-tight T-shirt as well as an old burn mark. He was writing in a ledger, which he closed, as we walked in the door. I didn't see a computer on the desk, but there wouldn't have been room for one with the guy's biceps taking up so much space.

"Can I help you?" he said through vocal cords that must have been dragged through gravel once or twice.

I began to give him our cover story. Without prompting, Bethany took over when it seemed apparent he wasn't responding well to me. I don't exude charisma, so it wasn't exactly a shock. However, this guy certainly liked my young, beautiful counterpart in the low-cut blouse.

"What would *really* help to give our piece a special perspective," she said while leaning over the counter and revealing a portion of her assets, "would be if we could talk to someone involved in the great work you do here who has definite knowledge of the conditions on the ground over there? Our readership..." she flashed a broad smile, "assuming we have a readership, would love to hear from someone with *hands-on* experience."

Thanks to Bethany's performance, I could have given Mr. Gruff another neck tattoo and he wouldn't have noticed.

He cleared his throat before saying, "I...we have several people who have spent a great deal of time on the ground in several African nations. If you leave your card, maybe I can see if..."

Bethany stood and made herself erect. I imagine Mr. Gruff already was in that state.

She said, "That's so disappointing. I have to travel back to Atlanta today and I was hoping you had someone here who not only knew the ins and outs of the operations, but *really* understood life in Africa."

Of course, Bethany and I knew a phrase like *life in Africa* was ridiculous on its face. South Africa couldn't be more different than Egypt and neither could compare to Kenya or Djibouti, but this didn't seem the time or place to dwell on political correctness and cultural awareness.

"I...I believe Mr. Hershey has lived in Tanzania," Mr. Gruff stammered. "He's here today. I might be able to arrange something for you."

I felt a surge of relief at hearing the man mention the alias used by Joseph Obol.

Bethany resumed her lean-in. "Oh, would you do that for me? That's so sweet."

He stood and returned what he must have thought passed for an alluring grin. "What did you say your name was again, sweetie?"

"My last name is Blane," she said. "But *you* can call me Lois."

Mr. Gruff, or whatever his real name was, walked out a side door into the warehouse area.

"Nailed it." Bethany bragged.

"You did," I admitted. "You're a natural. The way you jumped in when you saw I had no chance of developing a rapport with him was great. Not only are you observant when it comes to picking up a tail, but you're intuitive when it comes to interviewing and role play."

Back in the silver Volvo, Mr. Simons said, "Picking up a tail? You're talking about her noticing Mrs. Hackney's little helpers sitting outside her apartment." He allowed himself another chuckle. "I saw the video on YouTube. She kicked their asses."

"It wasn't just that time," I corrected. "I'll come back to that. But, yes. She kicked their asses. And you can use their names. We're old friends with Tyler and Kay."

Mr. Simons appeared to be perplexed, so I asked, "May I continue?"

Ten minutes had passed before Mr. Gruff returned to lead us through a part of the warehouse which wasn't nearly as busy as I'd been hoping. Other than four men walking around with clipboards and another driving a forklift, the space was occupied mostly by boxes of varying sizes. Each of the men tried hard not to look like they were noticing us and we tried hard not to notice them making the attempt. The full warehouse wasn't visible to us. At least a quarter of the building was shielded from our view by a set of giant doors that could be rolled back or possibly opened electronically. I remembered what Alana Hackney had said about the building having once been a helicopter hangar. Now I realized at least a part of the structure had been the hangar and the other part, possibly the section where we were standing, had been an addition built on later. However, the hangar doors remained.

Gruff led us up a flight of metal stairs that terminated at a single rectangular office space high above the warehouse floor. Gruff held the door open and admired the way Bethany's pants hugged her waist as she passed through. His eyes found mine and did not convey admiration of any kind as I moved my way into the office. Behind a wooden desk, too extravagant for the plywood and two-by-four setting, sat an African American man with wire-rimmed glasses. His receding hair was close-cropped and starting to gray at the temples. He wore a blue polo shirt buttoned all the way to the top and gold rings on both his hands. He glanced up from his laptop and stood as we entered.

"Hello! Hello!" he said as he opened his arms wide.

Although he was no bigger than me, his hands were huge and looked like catcher's mitts when he stretched out his arms and extended his fingers. The door closed behind us. To my surprise, Mr. Gruff was still with us. We needed to speak to Obol alone to confront him about the missing photograph so he would at least think we might keep his secret safe. Having company wasn't in the cards.

"I understand you wish to write a story about our humble efforts here."

Although Bethany was standing a few paces in front of me and was holding a notepad, he was looking straight at me. I didn't know if it was perhaps a cultural preference for Ugandan men to deal only with other men, or if he was simply making the sexist assumption I was in charge, but I decided not to rock the boat.

"If you have a few moments, we would like to sit down and talk about the great things Famine Assist is doing for those in need." Hoping Mr. Gruff would take the hint that he wouldn't be needed and would be bored, I added, "It shouldn't take more than thirty or forty minutes. And we were told you may be able to lend a personal perspective. You lived in Tanzania?"

The man stood and strode around the desk with one hand extended.

"I am Ben Hershey. But, of course you know that is not my real name."

I froze. Bethany froze. Neither of us dared breathe. Hershey, or rather Obol, smiled.

"My given name is Badru, but Ben is much easier for American tongues to pronounce."

The tension in the room lifted. I introduced myself as Jeremy Duffy and we shook hands. He turned to Bethany and grasped her hand delicately, as if he were going to kiss it, but then gave it a polite squeeze and nodded before taking a step back.

"I am happy to assist you in any way I can. It is so wonderful that you have taken an interest in what we are doing here. Unfortunately, so few care about the misfortunes of others. It is a sad commentary on our society, is it not?"

"It is," I said, hoping he would gesture for us to sit in the two chairs in front of his desk and dismiss his bicep-heavy coworker.

To help get things going I flipped open my own notebook, took out a pen, and made a move toward one of the seats. Unfortunately, my hopes were dashed.

Our host clasped his hands together and said, "Allow me and Mr. Gatlin to give you a tour of the facility and we can discuss the operations along the way."

Mr. Gruff, or apparently Mr. Gatlin, pulled the door open. Without waiting for either of us to respond, our host led us back down the staircase. The first thing I noticed was the men who had been working around the warehouse were gone. The second thing I noticed was the four-foot opening in the gigantic doors concealing a portion of the warehouse. The third thing I noticed was the sound of Mr. Gatlin locking the office door behind us. As if we weren't returning anytime soon.

FRAME 16

The rally hosted by the College Republicans at Robert Morris University had not gone as planned. According to the notes provided by Metal Security, the outdoor campus rally was supposed to be negligible in comparison with the others. The turnout was expected to be light other than a scattering of youthful supporters who may or may not remember to show up on Election Day, a contingent of unmotivated local press, and the usual participants-by-chance who happen to be walking by on the way to class, or to get coffee. The photo immortalized a scene much different than what had been expected.

Hackney, in one of his posh suits, had an arm raised to protect his face. Nick Van Metre was behind him, one arm wrapped around the other man's waist and the other pressing Hackney's head down as they rushed toward the open door of the limo. Demonstrators had arrived en masse and the university's ill-prepared public safety department was overrun by enraged students who had taken exception to the candidate's stances on the environment, racial relations, immigration, and most other topics. From both the notes and the photo, it's obvious the barrage of bottles and rocks was intense and the assailants were fearless.

One can see the outline of two shapes through the windshield of the car. One is the driver, ready to speed away. The other is Alana Hackney. She was sitting comfortably in the limousine, as if she had never gotten out. Fortunately for her, she had remained safe and secure in the vehicle.

"Would you mind turning off the engine?" Mr. Simon asked as he did a quick scan of the darkened Savannah thoroughfare. "I do hate to waste gas."

The street wasn't busy, but far from abandoned. Headlights would arrive and taillights would depart while the occasional late-night dog walker or student from the local art college would appear and disappear, unmindful of the Volvo. Every few minutes, I discreetly pressed the brake pedal, but not often enough that Mr. Simon would notice.

"You're an environmentalist?" I asked sarcastically. "Isn't that contrary to Hackney's platform?"

"Platforms. Agendas. Mission statements..." Mr. Simon scoffed. "I've spent my life watching ambitious men set sail in search of power and immorality while tying themselves to doctrines, manifestos, and philosophies founded in deities or phobias. When the sailing is smooth, they let the lines attached to their platforms lay loosely around their legs. But when the seas get rough, they twist that line around them for security and it coils like a viper. When the ships capsize, these men realize too late they have tied themselves to anchors and their precious doctrines are dragging them into dark nothingness."

The man's gun in his right hand bounced with the words as he spoke, but not in a threatening way. He was simply being emphatic. I had struck a nerve, but Mr. Simon wasn't angry. He seemed happy to have the opportunity to engage in conversation. I imagined he rarely had the opportunity to speak so freely about his thoughts. Of course, I knew the more he shared with me, the more likely it was he was going to shoot me in the face.

"Let me ask you this, Mr. Galloway? From what you've seen and heard, do you think Dennis Hackney is a racist?"

"Yes."

"But how could you possibly *know* this? The most skillful

politicians play to their base and Mr. Hackney knows how to play to his. Would it not be reasonable to assume a man may not be racist, but might shroud himself in a system of belief in order to achieve a goal, even if he himself does not hold those beliefs?"

"It's immaterial," I said.

"How do you figure?"

I didn't feel like having an intellectual roundtable with the man, but under the circumstances...

"A man capable of using hatred and spinning it for his own gain is no better than a man who harbors hatred. It doesn't matter if the person pulling the trigger believes in the gun. The result is the same."

Mr. Simon nodded.

"Besides," I added, "like you said, the ideology pulls them down eventually, regardless of the level of belief."

A corner of his mouth rose. "I just wanted to know your thoughts. I agree with you one hundred percent. But, one would argue that Mr. Hackney does have associates of various races and ethnicities. In fact, how would you explain his friendship with Joseph Obol?"

"His friendship from the past? That was opportunism. Their meeting again here was coincidence. Of course neither of them even knew they had an ongoing business relationship. You made sure of that."

Mr. Simon didn't react. "Maybe you should finish telling me what happened in that warehouse."

Now I knew I was either talking myself out of the car or into the grave.

The man calling himself Ben Hershey led us around the main warehouse area and gave us a history of Famine Assist's operations. Mr. Gatlin, massive arms crossed, trailed us the entire time. I took notes and asked basic questions about what kinds of supplies were sent out, in what amounts, and to what nations. Hershey rattled off statistics about medical supplies, nonperishable food shipments, and other goods that were purchased through corporate and private donations. Bethany chimed with a few innocuous questions of her own and our tour guide responded graciously. We were near the rear of the warehouse, examining crates filled with latex gloves and crutches when I asked him three questions. I didn't like the answers to those questions.

"When did Famine Assist begin operations?" I asked.

Hershey told us the year, which I realized was the year after Joseph Obol had vanished from sight and become an international fugitive. I asked the second question.

"And when did you start working here?"

He pretended to dwell on this. "I suppose it was right after the organization began operating. I was blessed to get in at the ground level and really found a home here."

Then I asked the third question.

"And how many employees do you have?"

Indicators of deception are a tricky thing, especially when it comes to body language. Not all people react the same and reactions are influenced by the environment, medications, alcohol, age, and psychological state. Then, cultural differences come into play. In some cultures, aversion to eye contact may be seen as a possible indicator of deception, but in others it is the norm. But many physical manifestations of nervousness transcend cultural boundaries. Before Hershey answered, he glanced down at his spotless shirt, picked imaginary lint off the front, breathed a little deeper, and his jaw tensed slightly.

"On most days, we have twenty to twenty five here. However, we are between shipments at the moment, so we have what you would call a skeleton crew."

Since they had a decent crowd when Dennis Hackney had visited, I knew the part about the number of employees wasn't the lie. That meant either the part about *on most days* or *between shipments* was. That's when everything started clicking and I felt I was on the brink of an epiphany. But my train of thought was derailed when Mr. Gatlin spoke for the first time since he had taken us to meet Hershey.

"Sir, they should be ready for us now."

Hershey replaced a lid on a crate, clasped his hands together, smiled, and said, "Excellent! Please follow me. Now I will show you the heart of our operation. I believe you will be extremely impressed."

We followed him to the colossal doors where the space that had appeared stood out like a gap between two enormous steel teeth. Hershey filed through first, Bethany followed, and I hesitated to see if Gatlin would walk in front of me. No such luck. He did his best to issue me an *after you* grin and gestured for me to continue.

Although smaller, this side of the structure was a near replica of the other. Even the stacking of crates and stowing of equipment was similar. But, something about the crates was making the hair on my neck stand up. Then it hit me.

Obol. A warlord who *happened* to fall into an enterprise that dealt with exporting to African nations.

Alana Hackney's henchmen for sale—their expensive, high-powered pistols. Mercenaries.

When I'd spoken to Chase, he'd said Tyler and Kay were on Dennis Hackney's staff. Not Alana's. I thought he'd been confused. Now, I realized he was more right than he could have known. They were always working both sides of a contentious marriage.

In my mind, the black-and-white photographs floated in front of me. How many had been taken when Alana Hackney wasn't present? And how many of those when Nick wasn't there either? Perhaps these were their private times together. One in particular, the fourth one. The one taken in the limestone mine, stood out. No Alana. No Nick. If Alana and Nick weren't there to take a photo, then who took it? If Alana was telling the truth, which admittedly may not have been her strong suit, and the only people who took photos other than her were Nick, Tyler, and Kay, then that meant one or both of her henchmen were with the candidate even when she was not. In which case, it was likely they were working for Dennis Hackney as well. Perhaps they were really reporting to the presidential hopeful all along.

I looked around at the crates in the sheltered part of the warehouse. They weren't like the other crates. No labels. No markings. Of course they would be labeled eventually, but only after a few of the legitimate supplies were thrown in to help conceal what I suspected was already packed and ready for shipment. That's why none of the other Famine Assist employees were present. *This* was the lie Hershey had been trying to sell. They weren't between shipments. They were preparing a shipment but not all of the shipment was legal. Hence, the only people permitted to be at the facility were Hershey, Gatlin, and the men who were now moving in to surround us. I glanced over my shoulder in time to see Gatlin block what appeared to be our only exit. When I turned back to the front, I saw Hershey backhand Bethany. You know...even with everything that had happened as of late, until that exact moment, I hadn't even gotten mad. Not until that very moment.

FRAME 17

Although unverified through any independent sources, the four handicap claimed by Dennis Hackney earned him a reputation as an outstanding golfer. He and three associates were taking advantage of a break in the weather by playing a round at Oakmont Country Club. Hackney was sitting in the passenger side of a parked golf cart, one leg out. One of his party was retrieving a driver out of a bag on the back of the cart and the other two were sitting and laughing about something while lounging in their own cart. If not for the two Metal Security employees in the background, the photo could have been used for a GQ magazine layout. The security professionals were attempting to look clandestine in their own cart, while wearing significantly less-expensive golf attire. Nick was one of the men.

Everything about the image said "elite" and although photos much like this one make their way into the press, Hackney's blue collar following holds steady. There's no mention of Dennis Hackney's spouse being at this outing, and it seems unlikely she would ride around and watch her husband hit a white ball around some fields for three or four hours. Although the couple portray themselves as close in public, they wouldn't be the first political power couple to keep up appearances to ensure the train to office stays on the rails.

With his non-weapon hand, Mr. Simon rubbed his chin. "I

guess a little photograph of Dennis Hackney and Joseph Obol seemed relatively insignificant at the time, all things considered."

"I wouldn't call it insignificant. Nick died because of it. Maybe Alana died for it, but I think that hatred goes way back. Tell me," I said, "what was the breaking point between the Hackneys? Was it when you killed Nick or when she told Tyler and Kay to set that bomb off? The note from Chaerea claiming responsibility was a nice touch by the way."

Mr. Simon didn't speak, so I continued.

"I imagine the two of them had been sniping at each other for years and had tolerated nearly everything. Alana mentioned Dennis may have used prostitutes and tried to act as if it didn't bother her, but how could it not? She said Dennis knew about Nick and was okay with their relationship, but how could a man like him not feel humiliated that she was sleeping with the *help*? The best I can figure, things escalated quickly and Alana took it personally when Dennis had you kill Nick. She actually cared for him. Then Alana thought she was having her employees kill Dennis, but being loyal to him—or at least to money—Tyler and Kay told Dennis about the plot. He decided it best to have them detonate the explosion prematurely and allow her to think Tyler and Kay were still on her side, while mopping up some sympathy votes. It was a brilliant countermove."

Mr. Simon's expression flickered and for one moment I thought I read...pride.

"That was your suggestion," I realized. "Well played."

He nodded. "Thank you. It's not my first rodeo." He rolled his head around, stretching his neck. "Things got murky, but you certainly complicated matters even worse. *Is Galloway in? Isn't he? Does he have the photo? Is he as crazy as they say? Is he as smart as they say?* You really are a conundrum."

I nodded. "Thank you. It's not my first rodeo."

Mr. Simon explained, "Nick had told Alana you had the photo, but he was a sneaky son of a bitch. It turned out he didn't completely trust Alana either. He decided to hold that

144

photo back and keep it as currency. Too clever for his own good. Of course Alana told Tyler and Kay, and that's why you got a visit from them."

He made a *tsk tsk* sound as if it was a shame his favorite basketball team had lost the night before.

"Well, now I have to know. How in the world did you manage to get out of that warehouse?" he asked.

"I told you. They pissed me off."

Bethany hadn't seen the hit coming. Like me, she had realized we'd walked into a trap and had turned back to see if we had an escape route. After absorbing the hit, she assumed a fighter's stance and moved toward the man we would now call Joseph Obol. She stopped when the five large men drew pistols. There wasn't any of the silly chambering of rounds and clattering of safeties being flicked like on television. It was five professionals smoothly drawing five weapons that were ready to fire. Real life. Real bullets. Real death.

"You were stupid for coming here, Mr. Galloway," said Obol.

"I agree," I replied.

"We were told to be on the lookout for the two of you, but I really did not think you would show."

"Tyler and Kay?" I asked. "They work for your buddy Dennis and let you know Alana Hackney was talking to us."

"Yes, but another little birdie told me. I knew the moment you set foot in Savannah, Mr. Galloway."

I scanned the room. There was no doubt the room was previously used as a hangar. The ceilings were high and crates were stacked along the outer edges but the towers of boxes ended just below large red mechanisms shaped like giant bullhorns. The devices were spaced equidistant around the roofline. It had been a while, but I'd seen devices like those once before when working a narcotics case that led me to a military installation. My eyes returned to the yet-to-be-marked crates.

Africa.

Warlord.

Exports.

Politics.

Mercenaries.

Money.

"Weapons," I said. "You send weapons and ammunition into third-world war zones and funnel some of the proceeds back to Dennis Hackney's companies."

Obol's eyebrows furrowed. He had no idea what I was talking about. The man was completely in the dark.

"You don't know, do you?" I said. "Let me guess, you think you're simply cleaning the money through shell corporations and holding companies. Does the name G.B. Barnes Investments ring a bell? I bet it does. You lose a chunk of the proceeds as 'handling charges' or 'transaction fees' or some bullshit. It's actually brilliant. Someone connected to both you and Hackney set you up in this racket and didn't have the courtesy to tell you were financing a political machine."

It didn't take a body language expert to see at some point Obol had come across the name of Dennis Hackney's investment bank and that he had no real understanding as to where a portion of his illegal profits were going.

"Don't you see? *That's* the real reason that damn photo is so important. Not only does it tie Hackney to you, a known war criminal, but it could shine a spotlight on his money pipeline. This is about his greed, not his friendship with you. Your well-being is secondary in all of this."

Obol was caught off guard and seemed to be struggling to comprehend he was in an unwitting partnership with a man he had broken ties with decades earlier.

"I don't believe you. I run a business and you have interfered with my operations. Nothing more."

Bethany pointed a finger at Obol. "You son of a bitch. You got away with mass murder and now you're profiting from more killing. What's wrong with you?"

As Bethany spoke, she took a step toward the armed men and out of the corner of my eye, I noticed Mr. Gatlin slide out from behind us. He was shifting out of the line of fire, which was not a good sign for us. If I was right about the devices along the roofline—and if the things were functional—then I needed us to get away from the hangar door and toward the wall on the river side of the warehouse. If what I thought was true, then maybe we could create a diversion and slip out the exit door at the far end.

If. If. If.

I grabbed Bethany's arm, pulled her back, and made myself appear to be slightly off-balance. We staggered four feet to our right and ended up in front of a stack of crates. It was a gamble on my part, but I was betting whatever was in those crates was more volatile or valuable than latex gloves and Obol wouldn't want anyone shooting in that direction.

"Don't shoot," Obol muttered to his men while holding up a hand. "Mind the cargo."

I started pushing Bethany to the right and she didn't resist. It's hard to give commands while processing information, so I decided to get Obol talking to get his mind occupied.

"What about the photo?" I asked Obol, while Bethany and I sidestepped. All the guns were still trained on us. In fact, Mr. Gatlin now had a pistol pointed straight at my head.

"What about it?"

Bethany played along. "Do you have it? Did you kill Nick Van Metre?"

Obol smiled. We all sidestepped. Fifteen yards to the wall on the river side of the warehouse. But would *it* be there?

"I've been assured Mr. Van Metre surrendered that photograph and it was promptly destroyed. I'm afraid your visit here was for nothing and yet it will cost you dearly."

"You were lied to," I said. "Who told you it had been destroyed?"

Obol didn't answer. Ten more yards to the wall.

"Fine. Did they tell you Tyler and Kay helped to recover the photo? If so, why did they try to strong arm me *after* Nick was killed?"

Obol didn't blink. "You are lying, Mr. Galloway. I have heard much about you. This seems beneath you."

"It's true!" shouted Bethany. "They impersonated police officers and even took a shot at him. They didn't have the photo. Whoever told you Nick gave up the photo was lying to you."

The smile faded from Obol's lips.

"They never got the photo and you're financing a presidential run with your gun money. It kind of makes you wonder what else you haven't been told. Doesn't it?" Bethany asked rhetorically.

Five yards to the wall. I turned my head. I didn't see what I had been hoping to find. Goddamn it! I didn't see it.

Obol shook his head and his expression turned menacing. "You are missing the point. Photograph or no photograph...it makes no difference to me now."

We arrived at the corner. Nothing. It wasn't here. What I needed had either been removed or was...blocked by the crates stacked inches from the wall. I moved back until my heels hit steel and tried to see around Bethany and behind the second crate up. There. The casing of panel on the wall. A metal casing, the kind that protects wires, ran down into its top. However, this wasn't a fully functional hangar, so I had no idea if the system was active.

"Of course it makes a difference," Bethany replied. "You can't afford for your picture to be circulated. You're wanted for war crimes."

"But you are here," said Obol. "You know who I am. Which means..."

I stood in front of Bethany as if I was trying to protect her. Actually, we were no longer standing in front of crates filled with weapons and ammunition, so the move would have been natural on my part since the one thing deterring the men from shooting was gone. All I could do was talk and hope.

"It means you have to move on anyway," I said. "You don't know who we've talked to and what we've written down. You're done here."

He nodded.

I took another sidestep and positioned myself between Bethany and the crate. It looked like there was just enough room for me to slide my arm between the box and the panel on the wall. Probably. Possibly.

"So you see, because of you I must once again start over and create a new life. Now it is time to box up your bodies and drop them into the sea."

Obol took several steps back to get clear as the other men raised their weapons to eye level. Quickly, I made my move and slid my arm between the crate and the wall making sure my palm was facing the panel. My forearm made it several inches past the edge of the crate, but the motion stopped at my elbow. The space was too tight. Now my arm was pinned. I was stuck. Awesome.

Obol and the armed men stared at me. Bethany turned and stared at me.

"Trevor?" she said.

"Hold on."

An awkward moment passed as everyone involved watched the Tin Man turn to rust.

Obol opened his mouth to give the order, but hesitated when I reached up with my left arm and used all my strength to topple the crate off the forklift. The wood clattered on the concrete floor, the lid flew off, and out spilled four Dragunov sniper rifles and several boxes of ammunition labeled 7.62x54mm API. I knew the Dragunov was a sniper rifle and I was betting it fired the type of ammo that was boxed up with them. Unfortunately, there wasn't a chance in hell I'd be able to load one of those rifles before Bethany and I died in a hail of gunfire. I decided to stick with my original bad plan and lunged for the wall panel. I blindly felt for a button, pressed, and a siren sounded. Everyone's heads swiveled.

Obol said, "No. Oh, n—"

Before he finished uttering the last syllable, each of the red fixtures along the roof started spewing hundreds of gallons of froth. The deluge fire prevention system, common in aircraft hangars, could completely fill the building with oxygen-depriving foam in a matter of minutes. Waves of the foam came down near Obol and his gunmen, disorienting them. The waves began flowing toward Bethany and me. I bent down and snatched up one of the Dragunovs and a box of ammo while shouting for Bethany to follow me. Two gunshots zipped past our heads and slammed into the metal wall behind us as we raced toward the exit door. When we reached the exit, I pushed the crash bar and shoved Bethany past me toward the river that reflected the setting sun.

"Come on!" she yelled over the deafening siren. "Let's go!"

Another bullet struck a wall somewhere. At this point, they must have been firing blindly toward our last position. I peeked back through the doorway. Three of the men were scrambling back toward the gap in the hangar door. They were going to make it out. I could see moving bulges in the foam as the others moved in that direction as well. Obol was wading his way in our direction, struggling to reach the exit.

He hit her, I remembered. *He hit her.*

"Run," I told her while setting the box of ammo on the ground and examining the rifle. I'd never used a Dragunov, but I could figure it out.

"No way!"

I figured out how to load and chamber the weapon.

"Run," I said again.

I took another look inside. The foam was getting high and now I could only see two of the men. Then I remembered the acronym on the box of ammunition. API.

"Run," I said. "Forget the car. Ditch your old cell phone. We're burned. Don't wait on me. You know what to do next. You were right. You were completely right."

She took off running. I was afraid she would fight me and

stay, but she must have seen something in me. She must have sensed it. It happened when Obol struck her. You can't forgive something like that.

I walked away from the exit and made my way down to the riverbank. As far as I could see in any direction, not a soul stirred throughout the industrial park. It was well after quitting time in a town that valued its free hours. I found a nice spot that sloped down behind an ancient retaining wall constructed from railroad ties. Obol appeared in the doorway, breathing heavily, covered in white foam. He scanned the horizon, and saw me shouldering the rifle. His eyes were hard and he stood at attention. He intended to die a soldier's death. I took aim and he braced himself. Then I thought about the other men who were getting away and how they had simply stood by while he hit Bethany and how they had intended to kill both of us. I pivoted and pointed the rifle toward another target. It was one I couldn't miss. Obol followed my line of sight and although he couldn't see around the corner of the warehouse, his expression told me he figured out what was coming next.

I stopped watching Obol and took careful aim, although one doesn't need to possess an accurate sniper rifle to hit a container in a fuel farm. However, it helps to have API—armor piercing incendiary—ammunition to ensure a detonation occurs. I pulled slowly on the trigger and felt the recoil against my shoulder. The blast from the tank created a chain reaction throughout the fuel farm, but the first casualty was the structure adjacent to the initial explosion. There wasn't enough foam in the world to suffocate those flames. The last thing I saw before the heat and flames blew me back behind cover was Joseph Obol being consumed by a hell of his own creation.

FRAME 18

Although he was at the theater, Dennis Hackney shouldn't have been entertained. During the intermission of the play that everyone who was anyone had been talking about, he brought his wife a glass of merlot, although Alana Hackney can't be in seen in the photo. The Metal Security notes mentioned she had rushed off to a restroom in a fruitless attempt to dab wine out of her white gown. Seconds before the photo had been snapped, her husband had accidentally spilled most of the contents of the glass he'd been carrying over a dress she'd bought specifically for the occasion. Although there were people everywhere, nobody else was standing in close proximity to Dennis Hackney at that moment in the lobby of the Benedum Center. If he'd been bumped, the other individual was gone. If he'd tripped, it had been over his own feet. Regardless of the cause, his reaction was incongruous with the situation. It could be due to the unfortunate timing of the photo, but it seems there is a hint of a smirk on the man's face.

As I finished recounting the events at the warehouse, I watched Mr. Simon's face as he processed what I was telling him. He wasn't a stupid man and he got it immediately.

"You told Bethany to ditch her phone. Her *old* phone."

I didn't answer. The growing intensity in his facial muscles betrayed his concern. When a man isn't used to expressing worry, he hasn't had much practice in its concealment.

"You told her not to go back to the car. That you were burned. That she was right about...something."

I started to press the brake pedal one more time, but saw it wouldn't be necessary.

"I see hallucinations," I explained. "But, if you are as thorough as I think you are, then you probably knew that about me."

He nodded.

"I don't trust myself," I explained. "As a matter of fact, I once nearly got myself killed because what I thought was a hallucination tried to shoot me in the head."

Mr. Simon relaxed a little and said, "Mr. Galloway. I assure you I am very real."

"I have no doubt. But you underestimate your opposition and that is one of your two weak spots."

He readjusted his grip on the gun. "I haven't underestimated you at all. Actually, I have a great deal of respect for you. However, I will admit to being a little disappointed at how easy it was to get you in this position of disadvantage."

I shook my head slowly. He tensed.

"What did you mean when you told her to get rid of the old phone? Why did you tell her you were burned?"

I turned off the engine, took the key out of the ignition, and held it in my right hand. His gaze followed my movements.

"When Bethany and I met with Alana Hackney, she said something that really stuck with me. She told me she wasn't a micromanager like her husband."

"So?"

"Have you ever met a person claiming to not be micromanager who didn't end up being one?"

"Point taken. You thought you might be tracked somehow through your phones."

"If things went bad, then I wanted a Plan B."

He thought about this for a long while. "What's next? You tell me you've been recording this conversation with your new phone? Or that you somehow phoned the police?"

Mr. Simon started to look around, but I tossed the key up on the dashboard. It clattered and he jerked his head back toward me, which is what I wanted.

"No. But that leads me to your other weakness. You don't know how to operate as a team. I get it. I've been that way for a long time, but I'm learning. You see, when I told Bethany about my problem with hallucinations and not being able to identify legitimate threats, do you know what she told me?"

"That your PTSD is beyond severe?"

"After that."

"No."

"She told me she'd be my eyes."

"Touching."

"See. Now we're back to your first weakness. Underestimating people. She tagged this Volvo tailing us as soon as we left the airport and then several times as we were sightseeing. In fact, it was originally her idea that if things went bad we would split up and rely upon our phones' GPS to find each other. Our new phones, that is."

Now he was completely off-balance. Whatever he had been expecting, this wasn't it.

"When I told her she was right, I meant about us being followed. When Obol told us someone had informed him as soon as we had landed, that left no doubt. She was right. And she's tough as nails. I wasn't completely certain until now, but I suspected you didn't have her. You'd have to shoot her on the street, because she'd put up a hell of a battle if someone tried to go toe-to-toe with her.

"We knew you were following us when we arrived at the warehouse and you would probably keep following me if we had to separate. All Bethany had to do to find me was track a little green dot on her cell phone screen. Of course I made sure she could find our exact location once she got close. I left the engine running and flashed the brake lights from time to time. I can't imagine it was too hard to find us."

Mr. Simon squinted and tucked his gun hand in toward his body to protect it. He started scanning the street in front of us. Empty. He looked behind the car. Empty. In the darkness, slivers of light reflected off his gun and his titanium ring as he tried to turn his head back and forth without moving his entire body.

"As someone once told me," I said through gritted teeth. "Savannah is a wonderful place to hang out, but a *lousy* place to hide out."

At that moment, the window behind Mr. Simon shattered and everything for him went dark.

Mr. Simon blinked awake. He tried to raise a hand to touch the wound on the back of his head, but found his arm wouldn't respond. The brick Bethany had put through the car window and into the back of his head had created trauma, but nothing more than a concussion. He blinked again, this time hard and heavy, trying to clear the cobwebs. Turning his head from side to side, he began to comprehend his situation.

"Just as I planned." He chuckled. "We ended up in my office after all."

Bethany and I were leaning against his desk, arms crossed. Mr. Simon was seated in the center of his second floor office, bound securely to a rolling chair. It had taken us a while to tie his hands and feet with the computer cables and phone cords that had been lying around. It looks easy on television, but I'd always used handcuffs anytime I'd had to restrain someone. *Confinement by Office Supplies* wasn't a course taught at the academy. Figuring out which office was his primary one had been easy since it was the only one furnished. Carrying him inside had taken a joint effort and quick action during a moment when the street out front was completely abandoned. Hauling his unconscious body up the stairs had been a colossal pain the ass. The key to the office had been in Mr. Simon's pocket and, although there was a panel for a security system, it seemed the fixer for Dennis Hackney hadn't set the alarm. Once we were inside and had tied Mr. Simon to the chair, we had a few minutes to spare until he woke, so Bethany ran an errand. Now she was back and not in a good mood.

"You lied," said Bethany.

"I don't believe we've met," replied our captive. "I'm…" He looked at me. "Forgive me. In all the excitement, I seem to have forgotten…"

"Mr. Simon," I said helpfully.

"Ah. Yes. You can call me Mr. Simon. At least on some days." He took a slight bow made awkward by his being wrapped up.

I couldn't be certain, but I thought he might have thickened his Southern drawl in an effort to crank up the charm. Bethany wasn't impressed and glared at him.

"I'm sorry, dear. You said something about me telling a falsehood. Did I say something while I was unconscious?"

"You lied to Obol."

"Could you be more specific?

"You never destroyed the photo."

Mr. Simon stretched his legs out and examined the bindings around his ankles. "Oh, that. I was afraid he would catch wind of the entire photo fiasco and send his people up to Pittsburgh. As you discovered, his crew is more sledgehammer than scalpel. It was best to put his mind at ease."

Bethany pushed off the desk and put a finger in Mr. Simon's face. "You're going to do two things. You're going to give us the location of that photo and help us clear our names."

Mr. Simon turned up a crooked smile and said, "Look, darlin'—"

Bethany whacked him across the jaw with a right cross. The chair swiveled around with the punch. When he rotated back, Mr. Simon's eyes found mine.

"I like her!" he exclaimed.

Bethany reared back for another punch.

"Wait," I said. "No use in breaking your hand. That won't work."

"Mr. Galloway is correct," said Mr. Simon. "Besides, I couldn't help you even if I were so inclined."

"Yes, you could," I said.

He shook his head. I saw blood running down the back of his neck from where the brick had hit him.

"First, you're going to give us the photo of Hackney and Obol. That will give us some leverage."

"Except, I don't have the photo."

"Yes, you do."

His expression hardened.

I said, "You've had it nearly from the beginning. You took it during the break-in at Nick's house and decided to keep it as an ace up your sleeve."

"And do what with it?" Mr. Simon scoffed. "Blackmail him? With what I know about Dennis Hackney, I could do that anytime I wanted."

"Maybe it was extra insurance," I said. "Something he would have to think about. Something in the back of his mind if he ever started to get the notion you were expendable. Or maybe you realized you could sell it. If he wins the election, what would his enemies—foreign or domestic—pay for a photo of him consorting with an arms-dealing warlord?"

The room fell silent for a long moment.

"All of this for a damn photo," Bethany said.

"Oh, swee—" he caught himself. "Oh, Bethany. You two entered the theater on the final act of a long, long play."

"Explain," I said.

Mr. Simon tried to adjust himself in the seat the best he could and gave us a brief history of Dennis and Alana Hackney.

FRAME 19

The biggest names in politics don't arrive at the Connecticut Avenue entrance of the Mayflower Hotel in the northwest quadrant of Washington, DC. They don't get ushered in the slightly less busy Seventeenth Street entrance either. The truly elite—the presidents, the prime ministers, the dignitaries who are under constant threat of assassination, use the tight alley just off Seventeenth and make a near-ninety-degree bend to the left before continuing to L Street. Once their motorcade comes to a stop, VIPs slip through a service entrance and into an awaiting elevator that whisks the protectee straight to the penthouse.

Dennis Hackney hadn't reached that level...yet. He needed to be seen more than protected. In spite of Metal Security requesting to use the arrival point in the alley, Hackney had insisted his small motorcade roll down Connecticut Avenue and stop in front of the main entrance. From there, he would march straight through the lobby, in sight of all of DC's power players and certainly several cameras. The presidential hopeful was in town for a luncheon with several Republican National Committee leaders and, as he was rising in the polls, it was expected many key members would come out in support of his candidacy in advance of several important primaries. He could have had his staff book a room at one of the hotels next to the White House—the Hay-Adams, or perhaps The Willard—but some in the press might claim he was being presumptuous. Besides, the Mayflower had nicer rooms.

Hackney's plan to be visible worked. All eyes were on him and his security contingent as he stood in the middle of the lobby. However, the black-and-white photo provided by Nick captured Hackney having a tense conversation with a man identified by Metal Security as a member of the security team. According to the notes, the security operative had arrived at the Mayflower thirty minutes before Hackney in order to check in to the room. This was protocol, as the room would be swept for threats before the candidate would enter. When the representative from Metal Security arrived, he had been told someone from the campaign had cancelled the reservation for the penthouse. Not long after—actually, immediately following the cancellation— the penthouse had been booked by another party. The security team member had made some calls to the campaign staff, thinking maybe Hackney had changed his mind about where he was going to stay. It wouldn't have been the first time he'd called an audible without telling his security detail. But the security member was unable to find anyone who had cancelled the reservation. By the time he had contacted Nick Van Metre to let him know of the predicament, the motorcade had arrived and Dennis Hackney was in the lobby.

The Metal Security notes went on to explain that the events of the day would be reviewed to find out where the breakdown in communications occurred. Due to the negative press coverage Mr. Hackney experienced, Metal Security would reassess all of the company's procedures to find more effective ways of communicating issues with staff members in the future. Additionally, Metal Security would seek to ensure reservations could not be cancelled or changed inadvertently or by unknown parties.

"Where should I start with Dennis and Alana?" he asked.

"Where all tragic tales begin," I told him. "When the screams of their reality became louder than the fantasy they whispered to themselves."

"Then we have to go several years back."

Bethany circled behind him. "Go with the abridged version," she threatened.

"Is she going to shoot me and ruin a perfectly good story?" Mr. Simon asked.

Bethany completed the circle and Mr. Simon looked her up and down. Then he examined my hands.

"Speaking of shooting...where is my gun? Please don't tell me you misplaced it. I liked that one."

"Start talking," I said.

He rolled his neck around and settled in as much as a bound man was able.

"I didn't meet them until after they were married, but my understanding is that while they were never a storybook couple, they started out happy enough. They both came from money and had watched couples much like them separate and divorce. I suppose they thought they were a little different because they both stayed single into their late twenties and got a few youthful dalliances out of their systems before tying the knot.

"If anything, I believe they thought somewhere down the road they might simply get bored with each other. Perhaps end up in separate bedrooms, attend their own functions, maybe find reasons to travel separately. Dennis was always an ambitious businessman and Alana loved being a socialite, but there was nothing about either of them suggesting the possibility of a turbulent marriage."

Mr. Simon paused reflectively.

"Until?" Bethany prompted.

"Until. Until." He shook his head. "I suppose Dennis drew first blood. Alana had an interesting business concept. For years, she had listened to her husband complain about how his companies offered tuition reimbursement for employees, but the program wasn't being utilized. The company would pay for an advanced degree, but the employee would then have to agree to stay on for two or three years, or else pay back the tuition. It was a good deal for everyone, but few employees took advantage of it because not all of the company locations were near a university and online learning didn't exist back then."

I peered out the office window, onto the street. The Volvo sat unmolested—the glitter of broken glass on the curb. I'd swept most of it away, but the remaining shards sparkled on the rare occasions headlights passed by.

"As I'm sure you ascertained," Mr. Simon continued, "Alana was no dummy. She got it in her head to partner up with several universities to create regional learning centers. They would share a building that would house several classrooms, a couple computer labs, maybe even a coffee bar. Not only could the employees from Hackney's companies take advantage of the opportunity, but so could others in the community.

"Want to get a degree from Temple, but you live in Erie?" Mr. Simon asked to no one in particular. "No problem. You want to take a class offered by Carnegie Mellon, but you don't live anywhere near Pittsburgh? Why not check out what they offer at the regional center in Harrisburg?"

"I've seen places like the ones you're talking about," Bethany said.

"But you wouldn't have twenty years ago," Mr. Simon replied. "Alana decided she wanted to hold discussions with universities across Pennsylvania, build alliances, and then find the appropriate facilities that would be in the most advantageous locations. And that's exactly what she started to do."

I asked, "What wrecked it?"

"Nothing."

"Nothing?"

"Not a thing. She did a wonderful job gaining the trust of the universities. Not only did she have the attention of the state-supported schools, but private universities wanted in on the opportunity. They quickly realized there was a chance to not only collect tuition from kids who might not have considered taking college courses from their institution, but there were scores of adults who would be interested in evening classes. Alana had them hooked. All that was lacking were the facilities."

"Which she intended to find," Bethany said.

"Which Dennis Hackney had already built," Mr. Simon said with a smirk.

Bethany let the words sink in and then said, "I don't suppose he did it out of the goodness of his heart."

Mr. Simon shook his head. "If that were the case, we might not be here having this lovely discussion. No. Dennis pulled off a corporate takeover right there in the bedroom. He swooped in, took her ready-made educational alliances, offered them facilities at a reasonable rate, and became known for pioneering the concept of regional education and training centers. Of course, he tried to sell Alana on the idea he was only *helping* her by providing the resources and that the entire enterprise was a *partnership*."

"How did that go over?" I asked rhetorically.

"Like I said, Alana is no dummy. However, she played it cool after the initial eruption. The waters calmed, the matrimonial status quo resumed, and all seemed well."

I heard a noise out on the street and glanced outside. A car with a rattling muffler rolled by and continued to a traffic signal at the end of the block. The light turned red and I watched as the car came to an abrupt stop. The light changed and the taillights turned a paler shade of crimson as the driver made a left. For some reason, the muffler didn't make noise when the car had accelerated out of my view. I had been considering this oddity while my eyes tracked back to the silver Volvo. A slim figure stared back at me from the street with dead eyes. Lukas Derela smiled, checked his watch, then locked eyes with me. He seemed impatient. As if the dead have appointments to keep.

"I suppose it was about eight months after the spat when Dennis and Alana were attending the wedding of the governor of Ohio, Stan Lenton," Mr. Simon continued. "Of course, the event was a glamorous affair and there were hundreds of guests.

Dennis had been asked to serve as the best man and prepared a dignified yet humorous speech to be given at the reception."

Mr. Simon paused, causing me to turn my attention back to him.

"Have you ever served as the best man?"

"No."

"Me neither. Why do you think men like us never get asked?"

"For very different reasons," I speculated.

I glanced out to the Volvo. Derela was gone. However, something else had appeared. A black SUV was now parked at the end of the street near the traffic signal. Of course, I couldn't be sure it was real. Even if it was real, the area was largely residential. If anyone hopped out, I'd ask Bethany verify it for me.

"Well, while I've never had the honor of being the best man, I have been present for a lot of speeches given at formal occasions. Do you know where men always keep their notes?"

I turned to Mr. Simon and said, "The inside jacket pocket."

"Exactly. So, imagine Dennis Hackney's surprise when he reached into his pocket and his neat little stack of three-by-five index cards was gone."

"Alana swiped the speech?" asked Bethany.

"Uh-huh."

She said, "Even back then, he was an experienced businessman used to public speaking and stressful situations. While he may have been upset, I'm sure he was able to improvise and get through it."

"Imagine this," said Mr. Simon, closing his eyes. "Dennis Hackney stands on a stage in front of hundreds of people. He's handed a microphone and he paints on that cocksure CEO smile everyone has come to expect. Dennis believes he is about to give a brilliant speech in which he will wish the happy couple well while saying glowing things about the bride and his best friend, whom he has known for decades. Dennis surveys the crowd, takes in a breath, reaches into his pocket, and that uneasy feeling of panic starts to set in. But he won't show it. No. Not

Dennis Hackney. He'll just have to…but, wait. What's this in his pocket? It's not a stack of cards. There is one single index card.

"There on the stage—in front of God and everyone—Dennis pulls out a perfect white rectangle. In handwriting that is all too familiar, he sees the words, I FUCKED STAN LAST MONTH."

Mr. Simon let out a loud laugh.

Bethany said. "Ouch."

"Precisely," Mr. Simon agreed. "Dennis tried not to react, but Stan and his fiancée had visited the Pittsburgh estate the month prior and Stan and Alana *had* spent some time alone. All of this was running through Dennis's mind, as well as Stan Lenton's reputation as a flirt and a womanizer, when the sweat broke out on his forehead. He stammered and stuttered uncomfortably for a good thirty seconds and the crowd became uneasy. Dennis looked around the banquet room and felt the walls closing in. Everywhere around him, people wore expressions of concern. Except for one person. Right there, seated at the table he had vacated, was Alana. She just sat there, serene as could be, looking like the cat that had eaten the canary.

"Somehow, after several more excruciating seconds, Dennis regained his composure enough to stumble through some best wishes for the bride and groom, but the entire episode was a disaster. Later, people made excuses for him and said he had taken ill, but Dennis was humiliated."

"It sounds like turnabout is fair play," said Bethany.

"You want to know the kicker? It wasn't true. Alana detested Stan Lenton. But when he'd flirted with her the month prior the way he flirts with every woman, she made it a point to act flattered whenever Dennis was watching. She made every effort to make it appear that it might be possible for her to succumb to his charms."

"You think she was planning it a month in advance?" asked Bethany.

"Oh, no," said Mr. Simon. "Alana was the one who invited Stan and his fiancée to visit. She invited them three months *before* they came. She knew how to play the long game and she was good at it."

"When was this?" I asked.

Mr. Simon said, "Nearly eighteen years ago."

"They acted like this toward each other for the better part of the last two decades?"

Mr. Simon leaned back as far as his circumstances would allow. He drew in a deep breath before answering.

"It was a sustained war interrupted by occasional treaties. Their coexistence would mellow for several months, but then something would happen and one of them would strike. Maybe Dennis would do something to upstage Alana whenever she was the center of attention. Then, weeks or months would pass and Dennis would show up to be seated at an upscale restaurant only to find out his reservation had been cancelled." Mr. Simon snickered. "That was one of Alana's favorite attacks. She loved ambushing him by calling ahead to a restaurant or hotel, pretending to be Dennis's executive assistant or some other staffer, and then cancelling whatever reservation was on the books."

I turned back to the window and sighted-in on the SUV down the street to my right. I couldn't tell if anyone was in the vehicle and it was possible I'd missed someone coming out of it. I looked to my left to check the rest of the street. What I saw made my stomach tighten.

"Why?" Bethany asked Mr. Simon.

"Why stay together? Why not divorce? Who can truly understand the human mind? I tend to think neither of them wanted to give the other the satisfaction of filing for divorce. In their minds, to do so would be a form of surrender and neither of them can stand to lose. Or maybe they eventually became comfortable with their lifestyle of mutual destruction. I don't know. All I know is that everything escalated once Dennis decided to run for public office. Alana never wanted him to run and considered this the greatest upstaging of all time. While she could tolerate the prospect of embarrassment among the rich and infamous, the national political stage was more than she bargained for."

"Bethany," I said while looking at the second SUV I'd spotted at the other end of the street. "We may have a problem."

She wasn't listening to me.

"Alana was intentionally taunting him with the photos, wasn't she?" she said. "She lied to us the whole time. She wasn't trying to protect her husband at all. Nick took the Obol photo out of the pack to protect Dennis while Alana was the one wanting to use it as a weapon."

"Right on all counts. She even made sure to capture my image—blurred as they may be—in some of those shots. And regardless of what she may have told you, the photo with Joseph Obol was taken intentionally."

"The only way you would know about your image being blurred is if you've seen the photos," said Bethany.

Mr. Simon didn't speak. I should have interjected at that moment, but my thoughts were starting to swirl. Lukas Derela had appeared to me on the street. He checked his watch.

"There were other photos in the pack meant to taunt him as well," Mr. Simon said, no longer pretending he hadn't stolen the original photos from Nick. "One in particular got under his skin."

"Which one?" asked Bethany.

I was half-listening. "The one of Hector Solis, the Hispanic board member who was killed in a hit-and-run," I said, almost absentmindedly.

Nobody spoke.

"Bethany," I said. "Do you see dark SUVs parked at each end of the block?"

She moved beside me and put her face near the window. "So?"

"Do you see them? Are they...there?" I asked urgently.

"Yes."

Damn.

"A few minutes ago...did you hear a car go by? One with a

loud muffler?"

"I...I don't think so."

Derela checking his watch. Telling me I'm running out of time. The car with the loud muffler. The noise ceasing when it turned. The muffler going...

I looked at the alarm panel on the wall. Then at Mr. Simon, who had been more than happy to keep us in place with conversation while the *silent* alarm had been triggered. I knew the only reason for the slow response time was that the alarm hadn't sent a notification to the legitimate authorities. Whoever received the signal and was converging on the building wasn't bound by pesky documents like the Constitution or the Georgia Criminal Code.

"They are heavily armed," he said. "My pistol, wherever you have it stashed, won't be of much use. I'm a reasonable man. Surrender and we can work something out. You see, Mr. Galloway. I do know how to work with a team."

I ran over to the office door, opened it, and peeked out into the hallway. Nobody was there—yet. I waved Bethany over and she fell in behind me.

"I'll be seeing you soon, Mr. Galloway. But, I do wish you'd leave my gun. As I mentioned, I do like that particular firearm."

"We don't have it," I said.

"You left it in the car? That was unwise."

"No," I said. "While you were napping, Bethany took the gun that had your fingerprints all over it back to the scene of the warehouse explosion. It will be found there, along with the driver's license that was in your wallet and some strands of your hair."

The confidence on Mr. Simon's face faltered, but only for a moment. "A gun at a fire proves nothing and the driver's license is one of my many aliases. As for DNA, I may not be in any system."

"True," I said. "But once the fire is put out and the police recover what's left of the bodies, they are going to discover a lot of weapons and ammunition were in that warehouse. On the outskirts of the perimeter, where the fire department won't have eradicated all the evidence, not only will they find your items, but they will find unfired bullets from Alana Hackney's two mercenary henchmen. Not wanting to risk taking them through airport security, I sent them down here via overnight package thinking we might have to plant them on Obol if things went bad. Of course, it's possible those bullets won't have Tyler and Kay's fingerprints on them. Maybe they loaded their guns while wearing gloves," I said sarcastically.

"That doesn't prove anything," he said again, but the wind was out of his sails.

I stood in front of Mr. Simon. "It doesn't have to. The cops are about to be sitting on an incinerated weapons depot, complete with corpses. The FBI will swoop in and forensics teams are going to have a field day. Your gun. Your prints. Your fake ID. Your hair. Your town. Your connection to Obol. And now a connection to two staff members of the recently murdered Alana Hackney. They are going to run your background from top to bottom. What will they find?"

The color drained from Mr. Simon's face. "What do you want?"

"Where are the photos you stole from Nick?"

He swallowed hard, then nodded toward a file cabinet. Each of the three drawers had a combination lock.

"Top drawer," he said. "Folder in the back."

"What's the combination?"

He gave it to me. I fingered the dial and yanked the door open. In a brown folder at the rear of the drawer was a packet of black-and-white photos along with the negatives. I flipped through, seeing the pictures were the same as the ones Nick had given me—except one.

"Got it," I said to Bethany while sliding the photos into the back pocket of my jeans. "Let's go."

We started to run out.

"You have the photos. Will you retrieve what you planted at the warehouse?"

I paused by his side and gazed down on him. "You killed Alana, didn't you?"

He looked up at me as if the thought had never occurred to him.

"You think I killed her? No, Mr. Galloway. I was taking care of…another unrelated matter in Maryland at the time. No, no, no. Didn't you hear? You and Ms. Nolan here were the last to see Mrs. Hackney. That is, until her body was discovered by her loving husband."

Bethany moved back into the room and stood on the other side of Mr. Simon and said, "Are you saying Dennis Hackney killed his wife?"

Mr. Simon raised his eyebrows. "I have to hand it to him. He finally got his hands dirty."

Bethany and I stared at each other.

Mr. Simon said, "Now, those items at the crime scene…"

"You're lucky we're giving you time to get out of the country before the feds close in on you. Consider the head start a courtesy. Besides," I added, "you killed Nick, you prick."

He didn't issue any denials. Bethany and I exchanged another look and he caught it.

"She's not going to strike me again is she?"

"No," I said.

Then I punched him in the face as hard as I could.

FRAME 20

The Knock The Rust Off trek through the Mid-Atlantic states wasn't to begin for several weeks, but the unveiling of the tour bus near Point State Park drew a sizable crowd in Pittsburgh. From the vantage point on Commonwealth Place, the photographer was able to catch Dennis Hackney standing near the front of the vehicle. Hackney had decided to forgo a suit and was in slacks and a button down shirt, no tie.

A crowd is cordoned off and a small platform has been setup for when Hackney gives his remarks. Two of the security personnel are where one would expect to see them, positioned to the left of the candidate, far enough away to not make the candidate appear timid, but close enough to neutralize any threats. I can't see anything to the right of the candidate because of the way the photo is centered. Dennis Hackney isn't in the middle of the image. In fact, the bus itself doesn't seem to be the focal point. For some reason, the rear third of the vehicle is equidistant from the edges of the paper. Painted in large script across that portion of the bus is an abbreviated slogan used for the tour.

KNOCK IT OFF

The hallway was illuminated by standard fluorescent bulbs embedded in ceiling fixtures and covered by thin sheets of glass. There were two options out. We could try to take the same stairs we had traveled once before since we knew they exited onto the street. Although we hadn't seen anyone move from the SUVs, it was likely they had been waiting for everyone to get into place before storming the building. Mr. Simon wasn't the type of man to have a light response to a silent alarm. The other option was a stairwell located at the end of the hall. An EXIT sign glowed over the steel door and I hadn't seen another door on the way into the building, so I assumed behind the door laid stairs descending to a side exit. Neither option was great, but one seemed slightly better.

Bethany had been doing the math as well. "The exit down the stairwell?"

"Yep."

"Wishing we'd kept that gun?"

"Yep."

Gently, I pressed the crash bar on the door and a squeak pierced the air in the otherwise quiet hallway.

"Great," I whispered. "As subtle as a Whitesnake concert."

"Seriously. We have to talk about your obsession with eighties music."

The door moved forward and I could see through the gap I'd created that the stairwell was lighted. From what I could see, we would step out, make a right, walk down four steps, and make another right to continue down more stairs. Because of the angle, I couldn't see past the second turn.

"Hold on," I said. "Watch our backs."

Bethany kept an eye on the hallway while I pressed my hands on the door and stuck my head out so I could see further down the stairs.

Tap—Tap—Tap.

Each of the taps had been followed by a solid impact on the door. I pulled my head back, gripped the crash bar, and slammed the door closed.

"Go!" I yelled.

Bethany and I ran to the other staircase. There was no door at the opening to that wide staircase, so I had started to grab her before she ran out to where she would be exposed to anyone coming up the stairs. As I reached out for her, she stopped short, sensing how to react. Bethany crouched along the wall beside the mouth of the stairs. She took a quick peek by edging part of her face out into the open and then yanking it back.

Tap.

A hole appeared in the drywall a few feet across from our position.

Bethany stood and put her back to the wall. "Crap!"

Stairs blocked. Too high to jump from a window. So...we couldn't go down. Calling the police meant going to jail, which was better than ending up in the morgue, but they wouldn't get to us in time anyway.

"Follow me," I said, while thinking about the benefit of being in an old, closely packed city.

We ran back into Mr. Simon's office where he was still knocked out. I looked around the ceiling, which was much the same as the hallway. The drop ceilings were nothing more than fiberboard panels suspended by a grid of skinny metal rails. I leapt on the desk and started pushing the panels, making them uneven enough so I could grab them and pull them out.

"Lock the door," I said. "This building appears taller from the outside. I didn't see access to an attic, but if there is a buffer—a gap where there is some insulation—we might be able to get up to the roof."

Bethany locked the door, which wouldn't buy us much time, and started climbing onto the file cabinets and bookshelves to remove tiles. I pulled down three more tiles. Nothing but pipes, wiring, and ventilation. There certainly wasn't a clear path and there wasn't time to dig through the jumble of metal and rubber.

"I'm sorry."

"What?" Bethany asked, without stopping her work.

I pulled down another tile and said, "I'm sorry about all of this."

Holding the tile in my hand, I looked at her. God, she was

beautiful. She dropped a square and stared back at me.

"This isn't your fault. I'm a big girl. I made my own choices." She reached up and pushed on the ceiling.

"I knew this was going to happen," I told her.

Bethany stopped, turned, one arm still propping up a tile. "Look, I have to admit it is spooky weird how you figure out some things and we still need to talk about that photo of the guy killed by a hit-and-run, because I have no idea what you were talking about. But, you're *psychotic*, not psychic. You didn't wake up and know you were going to blow up a chunk of Savannah today and you didn't know we were going to get trapped in this building."

"I knew something horrible was going to happen to you. I knew…I knew because I did the one thing to you I had no right to do. The one thing that sealed your fate. I fell in love with you. If we aren't going to make it out of here, you have a right to know. I do love you."

"I love you too," she said as if she'd said it to me a thousand times.

I blinked.

"Come on. Do you really think I'm doing all this for Alana Hackney's money or so I can write the great American novel? Not a chance. You're older than me—and you look even older than you are. I hate your references to Def Leppard, Cinderella, and Big White…"

"Great White," I said.

"Whatever. The point is, there is something inherently good and fiercely loyal about you. So, yes. I'm totally in love with you."

I didn't know what to say. I stood there on the desk, letting seconds we didn't have tick by. Bethany pulled down another white square. Dust fell into her eyes and she wiped it all away and gazed into the hole she had created.

"Well…" she said with a smile. "Pour some sugar on me."

I hopped off the desk and ran over to Bethany. From the other side of the door came the subtle sounds of feet trying not to be heard. The space Bethany had found in the ceiling was large enough for us to squeeze through, but so dark we couldn't tell where it led. Taking out my airport-bought cell phone, I used its light as a flashlight and saw what looked like a platform slightly to the left and above the beam. Running out of time, I retrieved several heavy hardcover books from a bookshelf and placed them on top of the cabinet. Bethany made room for me as I climbed up. I used the books as a stepstool and reached up with both hands, grasping a slat of wood that I hoped would be strong enough to support me.

I'd been hitting the gym hard lately, but pull-ups still weren't my strong suit. Luckily, all I needed to do was pull myself up so Bethany could help push me into the darkness. I put my phone in my pocket, grasped the support beam with both hands and pulled with all my might as I heard someone try the knob for the office door. Bethany grabbed my legs and lifted me up. I was able to throw a leg over the beam and reach out for the platform. Once I was able to slide my body onto the wooden platform that smelled like cedar, I gave Bethany my hand. It sounded as if someone tried to kick in the office door, which caused my adrenaline fueled muscles to fire so I was able to yank her up and get her on the platform. As Bethany's feet cleared the office ceiling, there was another loud noise from below accompanied by the sound of breaking wood followed by foot-steps and then whispers. We heard two distinct voices.

"Ceiling tiles."

"They're going up."

One of them must have checked on Mr. Simon.

"He's alive."

A bright light shone up through the hole we had created. Fortunately, the light from below allowed Bethany and me to see our chance. At the end of the platform was a black steel ladder leading up to a hatch. If the hatch opened to the roof, we might make it out. In parts of this old town, one might be able to jump from roof to roof since many of the buildings were within arms-reach of each other. However, if the hatch led to a mechanical room or was rusted shut...

From their angle, the hunters below couldn't see us on the platform but they knew we didn't have time to go far.

Tap—Tap—Tap—Tap—Tap—Tap.

Shards of the wood platform flew into our faces. Something pierced my neck and face.

Damnit.

We ran toward the ladder. Bethany climbed first. The light from below had disappeared, so I grabbed the phone from my waistband and shined the light on the hatch. Bethany worked a latched and pushed. Nothing happened.

Tap—Tap—Tap—Tap.

Beside me, a bullet ricocheted off a pipe and created sparks. Bethany turned toward the impact and saw me pressing a hand to the wounds created from splinters and shrapnel. I could feel blood trickling down my neck.

"Trevor?"

"It's okay," I said cringing.

Bethany took a deep breath, pulled her arm down, then propelled her arm upward, using the palm of her hand in the side of the hatch opposite the hinges. Until that moment, I'd never truly appreciated the beauty of the stars in the night sky.

In spite of my injuries, I was able to follow Bethany from rooftop to rooftop and balcony to balcony until we managed to climb our way down to ground level. We were a full block away from Mr. Simon's office and seemed to have made a clean getaway. We ducked into an alley and caught our breath in the shadows.

"We have to go back," I said.

Bethany was not amused. "You've lost blood. You're talking crazy."

"No. Really."

I told her why.

"Damn."

"Yeah," I said holding my neck.

"What if they left someone out on the perimeter?"

"We'll scout it out. If we see anyone in those SUVs or on the street, then we bolt."

Stray cats, perched warily on ledges, eyed our progress as we wound a fast yet indirect route back toward the building. We came up behind one of the SUVs and surveilled it for two minutes. Seeing no motion from inside, we stayed close to a home General Sherman could have once slept in and the two of us hid behind shrubs while watching the other SUV down the street. Another minute passed and we didn't see anything to make us suspect more adversaries were afoot. I used the bottom of my shirt to wipe my face and neck. Blood was everywhere. However I'd been shot in the head once before, so this wasn't that bad by comparison.

"By now they must have been able to wake up Mr. Simon," said Bethany. "They'll be coming out soon."

"Stay close to the building, so they can't see us from the window," I said.

"Of course if they happen to come out the front door at the wrong time, then we're dead."

"That would be the downside."

"Can you run?" she asked.

"Yes."

"Okay. Give me the key."

We ran and made it to the Volvo. Bethany got behind the wheel, barely able to touch the pedals. I jumped in on top of broken glass which was soon joined by more of the same.

Tap—Tap.

The rear passenger window shattered behind me as we sped off in a car we desperately needed. Bethany had gotten rid of our rental car and had overpaid a patient cab driver to track me when I was in Mr. Simon's Volvo. Since Bethany and I were wanted by the police and our faces were all over the news, we couldn't rent another car or buy a new one. The train stations were a risk and no Uber driver was going to take us where we were headed.

The problem with stealing a car is that someone will report it stolen. However, Mr. Simon was about to have enough on his plate and the last thing he wanted was interaction with law enforcement. No, the Volvo was the best option we had and the photo of Dennis Hackney and Joseph Obol was the only chance for us to gain a foothold in the avalanche.

"We'll have to leave our luggage at the hotel, I suppose."

I nodded.

We followed signs for Interstate 16 West, out of Savannah.

"Where to?" asked Bethany.

"A drug store. We need pull the debris out of your wounds and get them cleaned up. Hopefully, the bleeding stops."

"And then?"

Bethany found a ramp onto the interstate and accelerated. She lowered windows on her side in an effort to eliminate the low thudding sound created by the wind ripping through the car because of the missing glass on the passenger side.

"We have to get to him," I said.

"With Alana dead and us being viewed as threats, the protection around him is going to be phenomenal," she observed.

"I know."

"How will we even let him know we have the photo? We could go public with it, but that doesn't clear us of Alana's murder. Not to mention, you're still a suspect in Nick's murder and we just let his killer slip away."

The road in front of us was straight and flat, unlike any road in Western Pennsylvania. Before long we would get to Interstate 95 which would take us up the east coast.

"We'll figure a way to get to Hackney," I said. "And then we'll have to use the one advantage we have left."

"Which is?"

"Everyone on God's green Earth is looking for the two of us."

FRAME 21

The ceremony honoring former city councilman Richard Wood was held on a rainy Tuesday afternoon. Although not part of the larger memorial service held in his nearby hometown, Pittsburgh officials decided a small event should be held in the city where he had become an admired public figure. The service honoring not only the years he dedicated to the city, but also memorializing his military service, was to be held at the Korean War Memorial on the North Shore. Pittsburgh's mayor was the keynote speaker, but since Dennis Hackney had known the departed, he was expected to say a few words.

Although the photo lacks any color, one can tell rain clouds are dominating the horizon along the river valley. The attendees, including Hackney, are in dark trench coats and standing under a tent constructed of tarps and poles. A handful of onlookers are on the grassy hill, looking down toward the tent and the Allegheny River, but the rain and the faded memory of the man honored has kept the crown small. There were eight people lined up under the canopy at the time the photo was taken and a man who fought alongside Richard Wood is in the center with the microphone. Dennis Hackney is three places to the man's left. Flanking those being shielded from the rain are flowered wreaths propped up on easels. On the left side of the photo, a few feet in front of a wreath, is a photo of Richard Wood. Printed below the photo is the text FREEDOM IS NEVER FREE.

* * *

I'd been dozing for more than an hour. We were on I-77, north of Columbia, South Carolina. Truckers and late-night travelers moved with us as we followed the signs for Charlotte. Bethany's face glowed in the lights on the console as she sipped coffee that smelled so good I could taste it in my mouth.

"I went to a drive-thru", she said. "You didn't even stir. "There's a burger and fries in a bag on the back seat and a Coke here in the cup holder." She pointed to the center console. "I'm sure the ice has melted by now."

"Your coffee smells good."

"I had to stop again just to get some caffeine. You slept through that too. Maybe we made the wrong call and should have taken you to the ER."

"No," I said, tugging on the collar of the red Atlanta Falcons T-shirt Bethany bought at a CVS at the same time she picked up a first aid kit and pain meds. "This will heal up and the bleeding seems to have stopped."

I sipped the Coke. She was right. It was watery.

"I can drive for a while," I told her, checking the gauze on my neck to make sure it was still taped in place.

"We'll switch when we get to Charlotte," she said. "In the meantime, you can keep me awake by telling me a story."

"I'm not good with stories. Maybe I should turn on the radio and search for an eighties rock station."

She shot me a sideways glance. "Tell me about Hector Solis. What's the deal with the photo that included him? And Mr. Simon said several photos were meant to get under Dennis Hackney's skin. What did he mean by that?"

The air in the car was cooling. With the windows open, it would get much cooler as we kept heading north. Eventually, we would need to stop and pick up some more clothes and a few other items. Fortunately, each of us still had quite a bit of cash from Alana Hackney's initial payment. We hadn't traveled with all of the money, but enough to be comfortable. Of course, by now the feds had searched Bethany's apartment, found the rest of her payment, and filed it away as potential motive. If they'd figured out I'd been staying with Chase and tucked several thousand away behind his stereo, then he was going to have some serious explaining to do.

"Alana got her husband to think this was a team effort," I began, speaking loudly because of the damn windows being open. "They conspired and came up with the entire Chaerea scheme. Dennis Hackney left it up to Alana to compile the photos and didn't bother to look at the finished product until after Nick gave them to me. My guess is not only did Nick have a set and the negatives, but Alana had copies made just for her husband. Once Nick had told her the photos were out in the open—with me—Alana would have presented them to her husband. Maybe she left a note, or maybe she wanted to see his face as he thumbed through the photos. But Dennis Hackney would have seen a series of shots, some innocuous, a few with hidden meaning, some a cold slap in the face.

"Aside from the photo of Dennis Hackney with Obol, which was unmistakably a frontal assault, there were photographs taken in the aftermath of Dennis embarrassing Alana. There were some with quotes written on signs or buses and, although somewhat subtle, those words were meant for Dennis. She toyed with him by including blurred shots of Mr. Simon, which she knew was his soft spot because he's the man who knows where the bodies are buried and has certainly buried some of them himself. Then, there's Hector Solis."

"Right. The hit-and-run victim," said Bethany.

"Also, he happened to be the only board member of *any* company run by Dennis Hackney who was not white."

Bethany took a sip of her coffee, lowered it, and said, "Are you suggesting Hackney is such a zealot that he'd murder an employee because of his race?"

"No," I said. "To eliminate the only nonwhite board member

he had could result—and did result—in unwanted scrutiny. How many stories have mentioned how he now has no nonwhite board members?"

"Plenty," she said.

"Right. But the photo that included Hector Solis was interesting. In the photo, Solis was pointing directly at Hackney. It was as if he was accusing him of something. For Dennis Hackney to risk taking out a minority board member, Solis had to have been onto something. The firm he worked for, G.B. Barnes Investments, specializes in global markets. Guess what continent is one of the primary areas of interest."

"Africa."

"You must be psychic."

"You're thinking Solis stumbled on to something involving the arms dealing."

I shrugged. It hurt my neck. I decided not to do that again.

"I don't know. Maybe. Africa is a big continent. All I know is Alana Hackney thought it was important to include that particular photo and Mr. Simon all but corroborated my thoughts on the matter."

"What the hell was Alana's endgame?"

"Power," I answered. "She knew she finally had all of it. While she always had dirt on her husband, and he always had a lot to lose, he's never had more to lose than he does now. Those photos were her way of telling him she could bring it all down in a heartbeat."

"But Nick betrayed her," said Bethany.

"He must have thought giving me the photo of Obol was too much of a risk. That picture was a real ace to keep up one's sleeve, and not something you'd want to give to a person who might lose control. He held that photo back, but refused to let Alana know for certain. So, she sent Tyler and Kay to find out what I knew and what I might still have."

I opened the glove compartment, pulled out a bottle of acetaminophen and swallowed two pills with my watery soft drink.

"This was marital chess and Alana wanted to put her husband in check," I said.

Bethany sighed. "Then things escalated further. Even to the point Alana tried to have Tyler and Kay kill her husband."

"But, they still had, and have, loyalties to Dennis Hackney," I said. "They worked with Dennis to set off the bomb prematurely and Mr. Simon had the idea of adding the claim of responsibility from Chaerea. Think about it. All of the sudden, Alana Hackney is hearing the FBI say that Chaerea is claiming responsibility although she hadn't planned anything of the sort. It was Dennis Hackney's way of reversing the power play! The chess game continued."

Bethany added, "And people died in this *game*."

"Yes."

Bethany didn't speak and I felt something change between us.

"What's wrong?"

She stared at the white dashes on the road scroll by. "*You* killed people."

I joined her stare. "You wanted to know about my past," I said. "If knowing all that becomes too much—"

"I mean you killed people a few hours ago. You...you destroyed an entire building. There were people inside."

The road bent to the right and for a short time there were no other cars in sight.

"Did it even occur to you?" she asked. "Once you had that gun in your hand—did it ever cross your mind to run away? To *not* fight? Obol said it himself, their gun-exporting business was finished. He was going to have to move on. You could have walked away. We could have posted information about him anonymously and waited for the authorities to track him down. There were other avenues. He might have been caught."

"He hurt you," was all I could think to say.

"You could have let it go."

"And then what?"

She turned her eyes from the road, puzzled.

I said, "I don't know how to do that. I don't know how to forgive and forget."

Neither of us spoke for a moment. Then I asked, really wanting to know the answer, "Do you know how?"

Her attention went back to the asphalt in front of us. Or maybe it was on what lay four hundred fifty miles ahead.

FRAME 22

The Metal Security notes stated minimal advance work was conducted leading up to the Spring Prosecutors Conference, a training seminar sponsored by the Pennsylvania District Attorneys Institute. Hackney's hired security professionals would have appreciated having more time to scout out the Westin Convention Center on Penn Avenue, but apparently not even Mr. Hackney had been aware he was scheduled to stand in front of those sanctioned to prosecute crimes in the state.

According to the conference program, which had been printed months prior, but not publicized outside the list of invitees, Mr. Hackney would be speaking about the need for harsher penalties for white-collar offenders. In the days prior to the event, the press releases had made the usual rounds. However even with a presidential candidate attending, it was not expected a dry speech to prosecuting attorneys would draw much attention. It took a few days for the story to gain traction, but due to Hackney's surprising listed position on the topic of white-collar crime, considering his standing in the corporate world and the questionable activities of many of his wealthiest donors, word of the event spread quickly. Alana Hackney herself had made the arrangements months ago, but had forgotten to inform her husband about the suddenly well-publicized event.

In the photo, taken at a distance, Dennis Hackney can be seen working his way along the side of the room, trying to make his way to the stage. He's practically being swarmed by prosecuting attorneys wanting to either shake his hand or take a selfie with the man who claims he would be a law-and-order president. Of course it's difficult to tell in a still photo, but it seems his entire path to the stage is blocked by district attorneys who can't wait to get at him.

"Turn yourself in."

"We can't do that."

"Then I can't help you," Chase told me.

"You aren't. Officially."

"I'm not at all. Everyone is looking at me for being associated with you. They asked to search my place."

"Did you let them?"

"Yes. But not until I stashed the money you tried to hide behind my stereo."

"How did you find it?" I asked.

"For a former narc, you're terrible at hiding shit," he said.

That stung a bit.

"I need your help one more time," I pleaded.

"No."

"You owe me," I chanced.

"You really *are* funny. You owe me ten times over and you know it," my detective friend reminded me.

Damn.

I was standing beside the Volvo. We had pulled off an exit and into a gas station south of Pittsburgh. The late morning sun was hurting my tired eyes. We had found a twenty-four hour Walmart during the night where we each bought new clothes, baseball hats, and food. Bethany had picked up a pair of scissors and hair dye and pulled off a miraculous transformation in the ladies room while I popped the lenses out of a pair of cheap reading glasses. As many times as I'd watched *The Bourne Identity* and shaken my head in disbelief as Matt Damon "hid" from his enemies without wearing a disguise, I wasn't going to make *that* mistake.

"This is our only way out," I said. "They don't have hard evidence on us for Alana Hackney's murder and they don't have me dead-to-rights on Nick, but there is no way they don't stack the deck once they have a location on us."

"You're sounding paranoid."

"You've said that before," I said, reminding him of a time he doubted the drug gang enforcer was stalking me through Central Pennsylvania.

"This is different. This guy might be the next president of the United States. For God's sake, man. Your picture is everywhere."

"Help us."

"No. Turn yourself in and we'll work this out. I can't take a chance that someone looking to make a name for himself sees you and gets trigger happy."

"We won't get seen unt—"

Bethany, who had been patiently standing nearby, took the phone away and spoke softly.

"Chase, it's me."

She turned her back to me and began walking away across the parking lot. I started to follow and although she couldn't have seen me, she held up a finger, signaling me to stop. I stayed by the Volvo and stewed like a teenager while my girlfriend and my best friend chatted away on my cell phone. She returned two minutes later and handed me the phone. I put it to my ear and began to speak, but Bethany stopped me.

"Oh, he hung up."

I dropped the phone on the ground, smashed it with my foot the best I could, then tossed it into the wood line. While I didn't think Chase would do anything to track my phone, I didn't know who might be keeping tabs on him in order to get to me. Better safe than sorry.

"It's okay," I said. "You tried. We'll have to think of something else."

"He's in," she said.

Through my useless eyeglasses, I rubbed my eyes. "What?"

"We're on. He's going to leave it where we can pick it up and do what we asked."

I watched her to see if she was joking.

"What's the catch?"

She handed me the key to the Volvo. "No catch. You drive. I'll use my phone to go online and make sure the schedule hasn't changed." She slid in the passenger side of the car.

I blinked several times and slowly walked to the driver's side and got in behind the wheel. With the thumb of my right hand, I played with the gash in Mr. Simon's steering wheel.

"Just like that?" I asked.

"Just like what?"

I put the key in the ignition, but didn't start the engine.

"I've known the man for nearly fifteen years and he wouldn't budge for me. You've known him for a few months and in less than five minutes you got him to take a huge risk."

Her shoulders moved up and down and she smiled.

"So he's going to—"

"Yes," she said.

"Even the—"

"All of it. Exactly the way we planned. We simply need to pick up the package. But to do that part, you'll have to start the car."

I looked at her a few more seconds before finally adjusting the seat and mirrors to my height. I turned the key and prayed that plan A would work. It had to, because if there was a plan B I hadn't gotten the memo.

The package was exactly where Chase had said it would be. I retrieved the gym bag from behind a shrub in North Park and nobody seemed to be the wiser. Bethany waited in the car; ready to sound the horn if she needed to warn me of any watchers, but not because of Chase. Although I knew he didn't like the plan, it wasn't in Chase's nature to double-cross me. Our caution had more to do with knowing our faces had been seen by most Americans who owned a television or read a newspaper. Fortunately, most Americans are terribly unobservant, so even our rudimentary disguises seemed to be doing the trick. Back in the car, I handed the bag to Bethany and we did a quick inventory of the items.

"This is everything?"

"That's all we should need," I said.

We both got quiet and watched runners dart through the park.

"Do you think this is going to work?" she asked.

I tapped the wheel with a finger of my left hand.

"Honestly? No."

She leaned her head back on the headrest, reached over with her hand, and took mine.

"I think I'm going to need a new job while I'm waiting to be discovered as the next great female novelist."

"No more bartending?"

"I don't think so. I've gotten a lot of material from the conversations I've overheard over the past couple of years, but that well seems to be drying up."

"So, what's next?" I said, trying not to let my voice betray that I had doubts there would be a *next*.

"Maybe what you do."

I wasn't sure what she meant.

"I think I'd like to be a private investigator."

"I'm not technically a PI," I pointed out.

"Well, I could be. I could get licensed." Then her eyes lit up and she squeezed my hand harder. "We could work together."

"Well, no state would ever give me a license," I reminded her.

"It wouldn't matter," she said, turning in her seat. "It would be my name on the door. I'd be the face and charm of the agency. You'd work behind the scenes."

"Kind of like a reverse Remington Steele kind of thing," I said.

"Remington who?"

"Never mind." I squeezed her hand back. "Sounds good."

"Yeah?"

"Yeah," I said.

We leaned toward each other, closed our eyes, and rested our foreheads against each other. She placed a hand on my battered face and stroked my cheek.

"I don't want to lose you," she said. "I won't be able to get over something like that." She put her hand under my chin and brought my eyes up to hers. "You don't talk about it, but you've had your heart ripped out before. Can a person get over that kind of loss?"

"No," I said. "There's no cure. The loss is always there. I imagine it's like missing a limb. There is no getting it back and for a while, you still feel sensations for what no longer exists. But, you learn to adapt and compensate. You change because your world has changed. You accept the tools that can make you better, or you don't and you struggle more than necessary. You either let people in or shut people out." I kissed her forehead gently. "I'm trying to do the former. I want to be a better person. I don't want to be lost and angry."

"And if this goes wrong? If I go in there and they grab me?"

I leaned back and looked her in the eyes.

"Then I'll kill every fucking one of them."

FRAME 23

Although the visit from former Republican President Theodore Morton wasn't an official endorsement, many in the press made the inference. The Metal Security report noted the photograph of the two men dining at a restaurant on Mt. Washington, over-looking downtown Pittsburgh, had been taken from outside the private dining room. The two men are leaned toward each other in conversation and no other individuals are in view. Their table is situated directly next to the glass wall, which allows patrons to regard the city's skyline. There is barely any light from the inside the dining area reflecting off the glass, giving the appearance in the photograph that Dennis Hackney is sitting dangerously close to the edge of a cliff.

"His schedule hasn't changed," Bethany confirmed with her phone.

She put the phone away and checked herself in the visor mirror.

"How do I look?"

"Amazing," I said.

"But, different?"

I hesitated. "I feel like this is a trick question."

"Do you think anyone will recognize me?"

"No," I answered.

Bethany looked stunning. With all we had been through and

having not slept in over twenty-four hours, she had somehow managed to race through a mini-spending spree in the Shadyside shopping district. Now she was in a white gown, heels, and held a small matching purse. She had eyeglasses as well, but she managed to find the type purely for looks with clear glass lenses. You would have thought she was about to walk out of a fashion magazine rather than a stolen Volvo with two shot-out windows on Palo Alto Street. I'd positioned the car so if things went sour, I could hit the gas, get the car out onto West North Avenue, pick her up, hop on I-279, and get us out of Pittsburgh.

"Remember: act enthusiastic, but not crazy. When you make the approach, say the key words first then do the rest."

"Got it."

"Do you have everything?" I asked.

"Yes. But I need to tell you something. I should have mentioned this before. I hope it won't make you think less of me."

"What is it?"

"I hate birds."

I stared at her and said, "That's unfortunate."

"It didn't seem important until now."

"Agreed. Look, if you can't get in—"

"I'll get in," she said.

She placed a Bluetooth earpiece in her ear and I checked the new phone Chase had left in the bag of supplies we had requested. I dialed; we connected the call and did a sound check. She removed the earpiece and placed it in her unsnapped purse with the other items she would need. We left the call active, so I would hopefully be able to hear what was going on. We kissed and she got out of the car. With no small amount of consternation, I watched her make her way toward one of Pittsburgh's best kept secrets—The National Aviary.

I sat in silence and observed the tuxedos and dresses flow toward the benefit. Everyone was paired up, one tux to one gown, which was going to be a problem. Bethany going alone was a risk, but we knew my going with her would be suicide.

Even if I'd shaved my head, which would have revealed a massive scar from an old wound, I would have been too recognizable in a town where I'd become infamous.

"Well I'm already here, sweetie."

Bethany's voice on the phone was crystal clear, but I knew she wasn't really talking to me.

"But I've been *so* looking forward to this. Did you know Dennis Hackney is going to be here? *You* have the invitations, remember? Yes I'm sure we are on the list, but I don't want everyone to see me walk in alone. I can't believe you can't make it. How disappointing."

I heard her let out an exasperated sigh and then a rustling noise I assumed was the phone slipping back in the purse. A male voice followed. Although the conversation was muffled, I could make out the words.

"Miss, I hope you don't mind but I couldn't help but overhear your conversation."

"Oh, it's so silly. My...friend," she began, and I could practically hear her bat her eyelids when she said *friend* instead of boyfriend. "He can't make it and has our invitations. We're on the list, but I'm being ridiculous and self-conscious about going alone to the benefit. I don't know what's gotten into me. I should forget the whole thing. I'll make my way home before I make more of a fool of myself."

I thought I heard a couple of heel clicks before the male voice interjected.

"Actually, I'm happy to take you in as my plus one."

"Oh, I couldn't possibly ask you to do that..."

"Cliff."

"Oh. What a strong name. In a world of Skips and Mikeys, I stumble across a Cliff. I couldn't ask you to do that, Cliff."

"It's...it's really no problem at all. I'd consider it a pleasure to escort you."

"Well, if you insist. I'm Christine Lancing."

I heard footsteps and an increase in background chatter as

they approached the main entrance, which would double as the main Secret Service security checkpoint. Intermittent beeping made it more difficult for me to hear the conversation. .

"Thank you so much for..."

"...problem at all. Are you...the area?"

"I live in Cranberry Township. I couldn't miss out..."

"...my invitation. She's with me."

Moments passed and I didn't hear anything but beeping, thumping, and chatter as Bethany would have set her purse aside for inspection before she stepped through a magnetometer. More rattling could be heard on the back end as she presumably grabbed the purse after it had been deemed clear of anything harmful.

"I assume you've been here before?" said strong-name Cliff.

"Actually, I haven't. But I just *adore* birds. How many do they have in here?"

"Over five hundred, I believe. There is a condor out back that is magnificent. Would you like to see it?"

"I would," said Bethany. "But I don't want to miss the benefit. After all, they do need to raise quite a lot of money for the expansion project. I must confess, I don't know much about the project itself. I simply heard the words 'aviary' and 'benefit' and knew I wanted to help out."

"They want to build an entire new wing...no pun intended," said strong-name Cliff, who laughed at his own joke.

In the Volvo, I wondered how good the odds were that a rogue owl would break free from a trainer and go for one of Cliff's eyeballs.

"Shall we head to the courtyard?" he suggested.

The sounds on the phone changed as footsteps fell on stone and voices became captive under a canopy.

"Oh, it's beautiful in here. Look at these lights. And they set up a bar over there," Bethany hinted.

Cliff with the lame laugh was slow on the uptake, but finally got the point. "I...oh. Can I get you a drink?"

"I'd love one. A merlot would be wonderful."

There was a pause before her voice, now more clear, came across the phone.

"I don't see him yet."

"Are you going to be able to get rid of your companion?" I asked.

"Maybe I don't want to get rid of him," she teased. "I bet he has money and a stable career. What do you have that he doesn't?"

"I'm wanted for questioning for multiple crimes and I think I missed a court-ordered visit with my shrink, so...by now? Probably an active warrant or two."

"Ooo. Sexy."

The sun had set over West Park but the pedestrian traffic was steady. Fortunately, I was in an active part of town where nobody was going to pay much attention to a man sitting alone in his car.

"More Secret Service agents are filing in," she said.

"He won't be far behind. Do you have your earpiece in place?"

"Not yet. Talking on the phone is more inconspicuous. I'll put it in when I make the approach so you can hear what's going on."

"Remember—" I began.

"No, I'm not going to talk about it now. Yes. As a matter of fact I did go inside and I'm going to stay for the benefit. Maybe we'll talk later."

I heard the phone being slipped into her purse.

"Thank you so much. I'm not much of a drinker, but today has been one of those days."

"I know what you mean," said Cliff.

"What do you do? Wait. Let me guess. You're an attorney."

"I'm afraid not. I own a chain of furniture stores in the area."

Wait. Cliff. Cliff Praknar?

Cliff Praknar's chain was the chief competitor against the

store where I'd been working. I didn't know much about him other than he was always one of those *Pittsburgh's Top Ten Bachelor* types. His commercials were horrible. They were the reason remote controls came with mute buttons. Suddenly, two things occurred to me: Thanks to being the subject of a manhunt, I'd probably lost my job delivering furniture, and I *really* didn't like strong-name Cliff.

"How interesting," said Bethany, selling enthusiasm.

"What is it you do, Christine?"

Questions like that weren't a problem ten or fifteen years ago. However, in the Google and LinkedIn age, instant verification presented complications when presenting a lie. Whatever she said, it had to be vague. Who was to say Cliff wouldn't step away for another glass of wine and use his phone to run a quick search? *People are so fucking paranoid*, I thought as Cliff talked to my disguised, fugitive girlfriend who was basically stalking a presidential candidate.

"I'm a writer," she said. "Novels."

"*Really*? Cliff responded. "Anything I might have read?"

No, no, no. What was she doing? This was bad. It was easy to check the internet for a writer. At least I hoped she would have the good sense to say she hadn't been published yet.

"Perhaps," she said.

Ugh.

Then in a softer tone I could barely hear, "But I write some fairly racy books under a pseudonym. You're not into erotica, are you Cliff?"

"I…I'm more of a historical fiction reader, actually."

Bethany let out a giggle. "You're blushing!"

"I suppose I am. I do have to say, you are inter—"

Bethany cut off her companion. "I'm so sorry. Will you excuse me a moment? There is someone I see over there who I absolutely need to say hello to."

"Of course," said Cliff, in a strong, strong voice.

I heard bumps and clicks as the earpiece went active.

"He's here. I'm making the approach."

I started the engine. If this went bad, she was going to slip out of her heels, sprint for the nearest exit and head north toward through the park. Even if things went well, she was going to be making a quick exit.

"I'm ready," I said.

"I'm fifty feet from him."

A voice boomed over loudspeakers. Thanks to the event being under a tent and having two blown-out windows in the Volvo, I could have heard the sound without the use of the phone.

Ladies and gentlemen: Please give a warm round of applause to our guest of honor, Dennis Hackney!

The sound of clapping filled the air and the cell phone.

"I'm twenty feet away. I'm taking it out of my purse."

I didn't breathe.

"Ten feet."

Hackney's voice rang out. "It's a pleasure to be here on this wonderful occasion..."

"On him."

I said, "Do it fast and get out."

Hackney's voice faded as Bethany's encounter began.

"Don't turn around," she commanded. "I'm Bethany Nolan. We have the photo and the negatives. We know about Hector Solis. Tell your boss we know he killed his wife. He thought he was careful. He wasn't. Ask him what evidence he missed. I bet it will come to him.

"We will go public if you push us. On the paper I'm putting in your right jacket pocket are the instructions for you to follow if you want the photo back. Follow the instructions to the letter. If you call the cops, it goes public. If you double-cross us, it goes public. If I don't walk out of here untouched, it goes public. Nod if you understand."

There was a slight pause and I didn't hear any arguments.

Now go. Go, Bethany. Just go!

"You remember what happened the last time you pissed me

off, right?"

What...was...she...doing?

"If you mess with us, Tyler," she whispered. "I'll kick your ass all up and down the street...again."

Point made. Go. Go. Go.

"Headed toward the exit," she said as she moved away from Alana Hackney's former henchman who we now knew had always worked for Dennis.

I pulled the car away from the curb. "On my way."

A voice I was already sick of came through the phone. "You're not leaving are you?"

Damn it, Cliff. Go away.

"I'm afraid I must go," said Bethany. "But thank you so much for escorting me tonight. That was extremely kind."

"I would love to see you again, if that's all right with you."

"That would be wonderful."

"Can I call you?"

"Absolutely," said Bethany. "Do you have your phone with you? Put my number in."

She rattled off a number.

"I look forward to seeing you," he said.

"Oh, keep your eye on the television. Maybe one of my books will be turned into a movie and I'll become wildly famous."

I intercepted her as she walked off of Arch Street and she hopped in the car, half-giddy, half-terrified.

"God, I hope this works," she said.

I drove south, thinking about all the things that could go wrong.

"Hey. I nailed it, right?"

"I'm sorry," I said. "You did great. You were born for this."

I hit the Andy Warhol Bridge and headed toward what would be the rendezvous location.

"What was the number?"

Bethany kicked off her shoes and made sounds of relief.

"What?"

"The phone number you gave Cliff."

"Oh. That's the number for the bar at Applebee's. He won't find me there, but they have a pretty good appetizer special going on this month."

FRAME 24

The last photograph in the packet was taken at a Lutheran church in McCandless, north of Pittsburgh. Dennis Hackney rarely attends church, as has been pointed out in the media, but has attended with more regularity since entering the political arena. He's seated at the end of the first pew. His hands are folded in front of him on top of a hymnal.

Hackney stares straight ahead toward the front of the church. His countenance is solemn and carved out of wood. Despite his infrequent attendance, he's no stranger to the church. I know from the media reports that not more than a few feet from where he's seated in the spot where he and Alana were married. She's not shown in this photo, but there is one empty seat beside him. One wonders if the picture might have been taken after she had risen to excuse herself for some reason. Regardless, there is an empty space beside Hackney. The obvious vacancy stands out in the photo.

It was on the drive from Savannah when we had discussed how to handle a meeting with Hackney. Choosing the location for the meet had not been a simple matter. We wanted Hackney there in person and needed to give him time to process the information he was going to get from Tyler. Bethany's verbal instructions to Tyler had been as important as the note that included the time of the meet and who was to accompany Hackney. We gave them until one hour after the benefit ended, no more, no less. The time would be getting late and we needed to pick a place that would be semi-public, but not too busy. It would be best if we were around people who wouldn't immediately recognize us and might not be familiar with, or care about, Hackney. Also, we wanted there to be a minimal chance we would draw instant attention from the local police but needed to stay within the city limits. We were also going to make certain to avoid going out to the middle of some desolate park because...well, let's face it, nothing good ever happens at night in wooded areas when surrounded by armed individuals.

Bethany had worked her way down our checklist:

A light crowd of people focused on other things, but not totally oblivious.

Minimal security, but not isolated.

Somewhere in the city limits.

After some debate, we picked the place. The SouthSide Works plaza was a square formed by stores, restaurants, and a movie theater. A fountain sat in the middle of the square, the meeting place of wide walkways that formed an X throughout the courtyard. The instructions Bethany had given to Tyler were clear. Hackney, Tyler, and Kay were to meet us at the fountain and leave the Secret Service protection on the perimeter. It was up to Hackney to convince the agents to lay back and I had no doubt he would raise hell until they agreed to do so. As for not being noticed, the chances of any of us being recognized by the few people having late night drinks at their favorite restaurant or catching the late showing of Fast and the Furious 22 were not that great.

We parked the Volvo in a garage off Tunnel Boulevard, knowing we probably wouldn't be coming back for it later. I had to admit, I'd be fine never seeing that car again. Bethany and I did a quick equipment check, grabbing the remainder of the items Chase had left us. We killed a few minutes by reviewing our plan. Depending on what we saw on the approach, the two of us would decide if we were going in for the meet. There was one thing we absolutely needed to see for all of this to work. Without that one ace, the entire house of cards was going to tumble to the floor and we would have to abort. But if it was there and once we committed, there was no going back.

"I'm going to miss you," I said.

"I'll miss you too. We'll see each other again."

We kissed, not knowing when *again* would be. Then we got out of the car and began our journey to the fountain.

We were a mismatched couple walking down the sidewalk past the movie theater—Bethany in her gown and me in jeans, T-shirt, and a baseball cap. A few people were out and we got a few stares, but mostly from men admiring Bethany. As the fountain came into view, we stopped and assessed the scene.

One black limo and a dark SUV were at a far corner of the square—not drawing attention—but not invisible. Two individuals in suits were beside the vehicles, looking alert and unhappy about being there. Whatever Hackney had told his Secret Service detail to get them to back away, it didn't seem they liked the idea.

"There. Next to the fountain," said Bethany.

"Did they change?"

From the distance, it was hard to see, but we finally made out the figures.

"No," she answered. "They didn't change clothes since the benefit."

We both exhaled deep breaths and Bethany took out her phone to send Chase a message, then went into her sent box and deleted the record of the message. We were on the clock. I adjusted the recording device under my shirt. Finally, I removed my hat and non-functional glasses and let them drop to the sidewalk. Now we were *really* on the clock. Might as well advertise at this point. If you're going to host the party of the year, then send out a lot of goddamned invitations.

I took Bethany's hand. "Okay. Let's go."

Dennis Hackney was checking his watch while his wife's former staffers, Tyler and Kay, flanked him. We approached and the three faced us. When we were within a few feet of them, Kay stepped forward and held out a hand, signaling us to stop. Tyler walked up, joined his companion, took Bethany's purse, and gave me a quick pat down. He pulled my phone, the one Chase had left for me in the park, from my pocket and palmed it while he began going through Bethany's purse.

While reaching into her jacket and retrieving an electronic device, Kay said, "We've followed your instructions. Mr. Hackney is present only because he wishes for you to turn yourself in to the authorities. He is concerned for the public safety and hopes you will listen to reason."

Tyler pulled Bethany's phone out of the purse and tossed both mine and hers into the fountain.

Kay waved the electronic device around Bethany while continuing to speak. "Mr. Hackney wants you to know that although he cannot begin to understand why you would have committed these crimes, to include the murder of his wife, he will do everything he can to ensure you get a fair trial."

Hackney stood in the background wordlessly watching me as Kay moved the device over my body. It beeped at the center of my chest. I let my shoulders sag as Kay stepped in close, reached under my shirt, and ripped a tiny microphone and recorder from my skin. In my peripheral vision, I thought I saw some people glance my way and do double-takes before mumbling to each other and scurrying away.

Tick. Tick. Tick.

Kay continued the scan and there were no more beeps. She tossed the recording device into the fountain. Hackney stepped forward.

"We haven't met. It would have been better to have kept it that way."

"Yet here we are," I said.

His face didn't show any sign of concern. No frustration.

Simply business. Dead—serious—business.

Hackney said, "I understand you think you have something that might interest me."

"We want out of this," I said.

Had Tyler followed all the instructions?

He studied me and presented a quizzical expression. "I'm not sure what you think I can provide. The authorities wish to question you regarding the murder of Nick Van Metre and my wife. I believe they also suspect you may have had something to do with the explosion that nearly killed me. The belief is you are not a well man, Mr. Galloway. I understand you spent time under psychiatric care and perhaps that is the best course of action for you now." He turned to Bethany. "As for Ms. Nolan, I can only assume she has been swept up in this mess by someone who has convinced her that his delusions are reality."

Around us, I saw more eyes darting and several tentative fingers pointing. I thought I'd heard the breeze carry the whisper of my name.

Tick. Tick. Tick.

"We have the photo," Bethany said.

He didn't speak.

"We'll trade it for certain considerations," she continued. "We know you killed Alana. As I told Tyler, and I'm sure he mentioned to you, you weren't as careful as you thought."

It was a bluff, but that wasn't the point. There was no reaction from Hackney, Tyler, or Kay. Each of them was totally unreadable. We were running out of time. By now, Chase would have made the call.

Tick. Tick. Tick.

"We don't expect you to give the police a confession, but you can give us an alibi. It doesn't matter how. Suddenly find a driver, housekeeper...somebody to say they saw Alana alive *after* we left. As for Nick's homicide, you'll release a statement that Trevor was working for you as a private security consultant. That will explain his affiliation with Nick. You'll either find an alibi for Trevor or pin it on some other patsy. You're also going to make sure he's clear of the investigation surrounding the explosion. You'll eventually pin the bombing on an activist group, proving Trevor had nothing to do with the so-called attempt on your life. Oh, and you'll be paying any legal fees."

Hackney's serious demeanor broke and he smirked.

"No."

"We have the photo," Bethany said. "You're with Joseph Obol in Savannah."

"Prove it."

"I can't," said Bethany.

"Because you don't have anything."

"No," said Bethany. "Because we stashed the actual photo, but I took a picture of it with my cell phone."

We all turned to look at the fountain filled with water. Bethany's phone sat at the bottom.

Hackney turned and stared at Tyler who swallowed hard.

"By now you've heard what happened to Obol," I said. "And if you've tried to reach out to your friend, Mr. Simon, you'll probably find him unavailable."

Hackney turned back to us, seemed confused, but then his eyes showed recognition.

"Ah. Mr. Simon. Yes, he does use that name sometimes. I have had some difficulty contacting him."

"He's on an extended vacation," said Bethany.

"I do hope he's not dead," said Hackney unconvincingly.

"No," she said. "He's a loose end on the run. But I would imagine he's on his way out of the country."

Hackney nodded and seemed to be contemplating his situation. "Since I would prefer not to have any question of negative associations come up, I'm willing to see what I can do in exchange for the photograph."

"A lot of people got hurt because of a piece of paper," I said. "You killed your own wife. *Your own wife.*"

Hackney leaned in and whispered. "I'm not a fool, Mr.

Galloway. The recording device on your body was an amateurish attempt, but if you think I'm going to say anything incriminating then you're either a bigger fool than I thought or even crazier than they are saying on nightly newscasts." He leaned back a few inches. "I assume you will want me to provide a service first and then I'll get the photo, the negatives, and any copies you will have made."

"Of course," I said. "Unless we keep a copy as insurance."

Hackney's eyes narrowed, but he was a businessman and knew the deal wasn't going to get any better.

He said, "I do believe a member of the household staff may have seen Alana alive after your departure. If that individual were to come forward to the authorities tomorrow afternoon, would that be a good beginning to our relationship?"

I spotted motion around us. Now the foot traffic consisted of more than dinner-goers and movie viewers gawking at someone they thought they might have seen on the news. It was subtle, almost unnoticeable, but the specks in the corners of my vision seemed to be taking up positions at the exit points of the plaza. However, they must not have sealed off all the access points, because a news van had materialized less than one hundred feet from where we were standing. I'd been recognized. Hackney had been recognized. We'd been recognized together.

Tyler and Kay picked up on the activity and moved in close to Hackney.

"Something's wrong," said Kay. "We need to go."

I looked over to the Secret Service vehicles and the agents who had been standing nearby were now coming toward us at a full sprint. Not comprehending what was happening, but knowing it wasn't good, Tyler and Kay grabbed Hackney by the arms and turned him toward the cars. Then the night came alive with noise and light.

Screams of POLICE came from every direction. Men and women wearing vests and windbreakers of all types poured out onto the plaza, illuminated by a media camera. Yellow letters including ATF, FBI, and USMS, jumbled together with PITTS-BURGH POLICE insignias as bodies converged on the fountain. Somewhere in the activity, I saw Agent Ross in an FBI jacket two sizes too big. He had started in our direction but I lost track of him as everyone seemed to be yelling for us to get down on the ground, which Bethany and I did in all haste.

As we were roughly cuffed, we craned our necks to see what was happening around us. Not surprisingly, Hackney was standing tall. As muscles and guns swarmed everywhere, he remained a sculpture. The Secret Service agents he had asked to remain at a distance were trying desperately to fight their way to them, but it was taking time as the plainclothes law enforcement officers tried to badge their way into the cordon of uniforms.

But Bethany and I weren't worried about what was happening to Dennis Hackney. Hackney could stand there looking dignified and composed all night if that's what he wanted to do. Hackney was a tank. You don't head out on a battlefield to meet a tank unless you have one of your own. No. If you're a foot soldier and want to take out a tank, then you sabotage your enemy's equipment before it leaves the factory floor.

"What are you doing? That's Galloway, over there!" yelled Tyler.

He and Kay were face down on the concrete, arms pinned behind their backs by several ATF agents.

"Gun," one of the agents announced calmly as they removed a weapon from Tyler's waistband.

"She's got one too," said another agent while relieving Kay of her pistol.

Someone I couldn't see said, "Let's clear them and bag everything for forensics."

"Tyler Clifton," said the agent who took the gun off him.

I hadn't known his last name until that moment.

The agent continued, "We need to talk about an incident in Savannah, Georgia."

"What?" said Tyler. "What are you talking about?"

The agent said, "We just need to clear some things up. Is there any reason your fingerprints would be on some ammunition at the scene of crime down there?"

"Wha—no! And I don't have to talk to you!"

A similar scene unfolded around Kay, whose last name was apparently Arthur, except she had the good sense to shut up after asking for a lawyer. Chase had worked his magic and contacted a friend he had at the local ATF field office. Chase had relayed how he'd gotten a ridiculous tip that a couple of individuals involved in a warehouse explosion in Georgia were going to be conducting some sort of meeting at SouthSide Works at a particular time. My detective friend told the ATF man he knew the tip was bullshit, but the informant had dropped the names Tyler and Kay and mentioned they carry serious firepower—FN Five-Sevens. Chase was sure it was a waste of time, but felt it was his duty to mention the tip. The ATF agent made some calls, and found there were some partial prints on unexpended rounds of ammunition at a major crime scene in Georgia. Once the ATF had the first names Tyler and Kay, they were able to limit the search. Both Tyler and Kay had fingerprints on file from their military service, so narrowing down the list of possible hits hadn't taken long. Chase's informant had also mentioned one other odd detail regarding the upcoming meeting.

The ATF continued searching Tyler and Kay while Bethany and I were checked thoroughly as well. Someone read us our Miranda rights, but we weren't listening. We were focused completely on the search of Tyler.

Let it be there. Come on. I know Chase called in the tip. Let it be there. Please!

An agent reached into Tyler's left jacket pocket and found the handwritten instructions Bethany had given him. The agent searched the right pocket and turned it inside out. Nothing.

Come on. Not inside the pocket. Come on.

The agent felt under the pocket and found a small rectangle clipped to the inner lining of the jacket. The jacket Tyler would certainly be wearing to conceal a weapon. The jacket we hoped he wouldn't have time to change out of if we timed the meeting right.

"What's this?" asked the agent.

Tyler tried to turn his head to see and the agent lowered the rectangle to the mercenary's line of sight.

"I have no idea. It's not mine."

"It's not yours?"

"That's what I said," Tyler yelled defiantly.

The agent said, "Then I guess it's abandoned property. Looks like a small recording device. Voice activated."

At that, Tyler nearly broke his neck trying to look up. I moved my gaze to Dennis Hackney who had overheard the conversation. His expression of smugness was replaced by one of shock. Now his face had turned ghostly.

The agent who found the device turned to his partner. "Watch Mr. Clifton for a moment, will you?"

The agent with the recorder Bethany had clipped to Tyler held it up to his ear, then turned and walked away. Hackney's mouth was open and his eyes were wide.

"You didn't discuss anything with Tyler before we met, did you Dennis?" I asked. "Did he ask you what you might have missed after killing Alana? No confessions before you got into the vehicle with the Secret Service agents?"

Before Hackney could react, he was swept up by his Secret Service detail, which had finally reached him, and whisked away to his limo.

"Do you think we got him?" asked Bethany as we were both pulled to our feet by whatever agency or department wanted a piece of us first. We had stayed inside the city limits to ensure a nice strong Pittsburgh PD presence, and they didn't disappoint. I saw detectives Gerchak and Langdale making their way for us. They'd gotten word and appeared to be extremely pleased to see us in cuffs, but I didn't care. I was thinking about Bethany's question.

I thought about Dennis Hackney's ego and his recent desire to eliminate any obstacles standing between him and his goals. Then I caught a glimpse of the ATF agent who was listening to the recording on the miniature device Tyler had been carrying. The agent was mesmerized by whatever he was hearing. At one point, the man lowered the recorder and stood on his toes until he found Hackney's limo in the distance. The ATF agent watched intently as it sped away.

"Yeah," I said. "We got the bastard."

EPILOGUE

Three Months Later

"This is awful," I said.

"I know! Isn't it great?"

"I saw a snake outside."

"The landlord said it might have been a legless lizard."

"That would be a snake."

Bethany opened a closet door. It nearly fell off the hinges. "Snakes don't have eyelids. Legless lizards do."

"I'm...I'm not getting close enough—" I began before realizing the insanity of the conversation. "It's a snake. And there might be a mold problem."

"It's coastal Georgia, Trevor. Things are going to be different."

That was an understatement. While we had tried to weather the storm in Pittsburgh, the media attention had become too much to bear. Dennis Hackney wouldn't even be going on trial for his wife's murder for at least another year, but the calls for interviews and the sideways glances on the street had forced Bethany and me to make a hard choice. Either we could stay in the Steel City and become public figures, or we could try to start over in a place where we might be less recognizable—if that were even possible. As the facts of the investigation had been divulged, we conveniently left out the fact I'd blown up part of Savannah. Chase had played along, so Bethany and I had decided to make a go of it in a town known to embrace a healthy amount of insanity. It took some convincing on the part of my attorney for the Pennsylvania court system to relinquish their supervision of me, but in the end I think they were happy to be rid of the burden.

"We'll clean it up, add some paint, and pick out some decent furniture. Before you know it, this will be a functional working space," she said.

"You still have to complete the required training hours."

"No problem," she said smiling. "I'd say I've already had a hell of an apprenticeship."

I leaned against a window sill that creaked. "That you have. That you have."

"We need a name," she reminded me.

"It's your agency. I just work here."

"It's *our* agency. We'll be working together."

While that might be true, we both knew it was best if my association with the company was kept quiet. While Dennis Hackney had been arrested for killing his wife and Tyler had made a deal to implicate the candidate in the murder of Nick Van Metre and the explosion that had made him appear to be a victim, I was still a known lunatic tied to a lot of people no longer among the living. Tyler Clifton ended up being a chatty fellow. Not only did he cause an assortment of legal entanglements for his former employer, but he admitted that he and his partner Kay Arthur had impersonated police officers in an attempt to find out if I still had the photographs. It also turned out she was tech savvy and had eliminated any digital footprint of my correspondence with Nick. Kay rolled as well and was helping to put Dennis Hackney into an even deeper hole. The one oddity shared between the accounts given by Tyler and Kay was that both made reference to a fixer Dennis Hackney had hired, but neither would give information about the man. Both of the mercenaries stated unequivocally that their lives would be in danger if they were to give any details about Dennis Hackney's mysterious chief problem solver.

Although both Tyler and Kay adamantly denied playing a role in the destruction of the Famine Assist warehouse and much of the adjacent fuel farm in Savannah, neither pointed a finger at me since they would have to then suggest why I might have gone there. They both decided the smart move was to deny any knowledge of the facility that the US government had determined was part of a major arms dealing operation. The photo of Dennis Hackney and Joseph Obol had made the cover of *Time* magazine. Of course, that's not where Bethany and I had sent it before the meeting at SouthSide Works, but the photo made its way around after arriving at the *Pittsburgh Post-Gazette*. I'd kept the negatives tucked in one of my socks during the meeting. While not the most elaborate of hiding places, I knew the FBI or ATF would find the negatives, and specifically the one of Hackney and Obol, when I was taken into custody. Then, I could tell the story. The financial relationship between Famine Assist and G.B. Barnes Investments became a massive investigation and took some unexpected turns. The early findings indicated the arms dealing operation was financing political operations for Dennis Hackney, but also for several other politicians, some of whom weren't even American.

Bethany examined a spot where paint had peeled away from a wall. I had no idea why she'd focused on that particular spot, since there were plenty to choose from in the old southern home.

My new phone dinged, indicating I had a text message. The message had to be from Chase since he was the only person other than Bethany to have the number. I dug the phone from my pocket.

"I've got it," she said. "Legless Lizard Investigations."

I cringed.

"No?"

"That's a snake," I said again.

I checked the preview of the text message. It was from a number I didn't recognize. The text read, *Trevor: Urgent Matter.*

"Coastal Investigations and Security," she said. "Or CIS, for short."

"We're going to do security work too?" I asked.

I opened the message. A video file was attached. Since I figured Chase must have been sending the message, I didn't hesitate opening clicking the link.

"If someone is willing to pay, then I don't see why not," said Bethany.

The video opened on the screen and the point of view was from someone moving toward a building. The dilapidated one-story structure had a few neon signs blinking in the windows. A scattering of cars and motorcycles was parked in a side lot. Everything about the place screamed *dive bar*.

Bethany walked up beside me and leaned against the window sill. It groaned more and nearly gave way.

"What is it?"

"I'm not sure," I said.

Whoever was carrying the camera walked closer to the bar and then to the front door. A faded sign—if you could even call it that—over the door read, *The Cask*. A hand appeared in the screen and spread out flat on the red panel door. Bethany and I stopped breathing when we saw the black titanium ring on one of the fingers.

The door swung open and the video showed the patrons all turn toward the door, none of them appearing to be impressed by Mr. Simon's presence. Without a word, Mr. Simon moved to the bar and approached a man in his thirties who had tattoos from his wrists to his jawbones. The camera panned down as a photo was set flat on the bar. The photo was black-and-white, not unlike the ones that had haunted Dennis Hackney. But this photo didn't include the former presidential candidate.

"My God," said Bethany. "That's us. That's us on River Street. That was taken last week!"

On the bottom of the photo were written the words, *Trevor Galloway—Savannah, Georgia*.

Mr. Simon exchanged quick, rough words with the bartender. I didn't understand all of them, because they were spoken in Russian. I didn't need to understand all of them to know what he was doing.

"Trevor? Is this what I think it is?"

"Yes."

The camera angle changed and we saw the inside of the door and then sunlight. The camera kept moving as Mr. Simon strode along a gravel lot. He never turned the camera toward himself and from the height I wondered if it wasn't clipped on to his shirt or jacket. In the distance, I could see the skyline of a city I recognized. Cleveland. He'd found an outpost for the EEDC and made contact with them in Cleveland. A Volvo, exactly like the one we had stolen, but with windows intact, came into view as he spoke.

"I'm sending this to you today. You gave me a head start, so I will grant you the same courtesy."

He slid into the car and got behind the wheel. I couldn't believe my eyes. The steering wheel was aligned perfectly straight and there was a gash at the two o'clock position. The son of a bitch wasn't driving a Volvo *like* his old one. Somehow he'd retrieved the car we had stolen and had the windows repaired.

He adjusted the camera so it showed his eyes in the rearview mirror. He said, "While the nature of our interaction was unfortunate, I do have great respect for both of you. Perhaps our paths will cross again in the future, unless your old friends find you first. It seems they are still extremely interested in you, Mr. Galloway. You are not forgotten by any means. So if you prevail, maybe we will meet one day. Until then, do take care of my former town." Almost jovially, he added, "I've always said, if you take care of Savannah, then it will take care of you."

The video ended. I put the phone into my pocket and Bethany put her head on my shoulder.

"How long do you think we have?"

"A few weeks," I said. "Possibly months. They'll come in

cautious, knowing rough-looking men with heavy accents and neck tattoos may not blend in here. Then again, with the tourist crowd and the art school, maybe they won't stand out as much as we'd like. Regardless, they'll probably send in two or three enforcers to scout it out, determine our exact location, and see if our defenses are down."

"They'll send more than one because you beat one of them before."

I didn't answer.

"I don't want to run," she said.

"I know."

"I don't want to sit around and be a good victim either."

"Okay."

"Okay," she said.

"So door number three?"

"Looks like it."

"How much money do we have left?"

"Enough to prepare. Enough to fight."

I nodded. "You're my eyes."

"You're my heart."

After a while, she looked up at me and smiled. "You could always go ask them for forgiveness."

I kissed her on the forehead and looked out the window.

"Maybe," I said. "But in my experience, that's a request best made with one hand extended in peace while the other is gripping something extremely deadly."

We held each other and listened to the nothingness that old houses tend to retain.

Finally, Bethany said, "Other than each other, we don't have much of a team."

Across the street, wild-eyed Lukas Derala paced the sidewalk. In the past, the delusion had tormented me and wished me dead. However, at Mr. Simon's office, my subconscious had used him to give me a warning that we were running out of time. In Alana Hackney's office, he had tried to tell me I was getting myself involved in a domestic dispute. Still, I couldn't trust him. Which meant I couldn't trust me.

On the front porch, Lucile sat in a rocking chair that she couldn't rock. She'd been hanging out a lot lately and had really taken to the Southern way of life. For the moment the black woman with the golden pipes wasn't singing or humming. No Elvis. No Billie Holliday. Unfortunately, my mind inexplicably had her dressing up like she was attending a cotillion. All around me, cars drove down the street, teens walked dogs, squirrels climbed trees, birds perched on fences. Some of it was real. I hoped most of it was real.

Bethany pulled me tighter and squeezed. I could smell something faintly tropical on her skin. Her hair brushed the side of my neck, which now had a few new scars, and my skin felt like it was being touched by angel wings. She was real. This was real and that's all that mattered. Losing her was not an option and if people intended to do us harm, then we would have to meet, and even exceed, the intensity of their intent.

As I breathed Bethany in and thought of what I would do to protect her, Lucile began singing. For her audience of one, she sang an unhurried version of "Livin' on a Prayer" by Bon Jovi.

Good ol', Lucile. She always knew how much I loved the classics.

ACKNOWLEDGMENTS

As always, thanks to the crew at Down & Out Books for their continued support and friendship. The writing business can be tough, but they make it…less tough. I'm a huge fan and a member of the International Thriller Writers organization. I don't know of any organization that does so much for its members and asks so little. ITW does a fantastic job supporting me and my fellow contributors on the website The Thrill Begins. We have a great bunch of writers there and I consider them all to be great friends. Special thanks to Steve Hemingway who provided me with specific information regarding incendiary rounds and many other things that go "boom". Any errors or liberties taken regarding those particulars in this book are due to my misunderstanding decision to increase the carnage. Thanks to Brian Hensley for cluing me in on photography and the elements of film development. For a younger brother, Brian is becoming fairly useful.

I do want to mention the U.S. Secret Service who provided me a great deal of training and expertise during my time with that agency. In this book, I took certain liberties that allowed me to make a presidential candidate more exposed than would otherwise be possible. This was intentional on my part. While I possibly could have used insider knowledge to conceive of more realistic situations in which a USSS protectee or his/her property, could be illegally accessed, I refused to do so for obvious reasons. So, if anyone wishes to use this book as a blueprint for how to get close to a presidential candidate—that person is out of luck. There is a reason this is on the FICTION shelf.

J.J. HENSLEY is a former police officer and former Special Agent with the U.S. Secret Service. He is the author of the novels *Resolve*, *Measure Twice*, *Chalk's Outline*, *Bolt Action Remedy*, and *Record Scratch*. He is also one of the contributors to the critically-acclaimed novel in stories, *The Night of the Flood*.

Mr. Hensley's first novel *Resolve* was named one of the Best Books of 2013 by Suspense Magazine and was named a Thriller Award finalist for Best First Novel.

He is a member of the International Thriller Writers.

Hensley-books.com

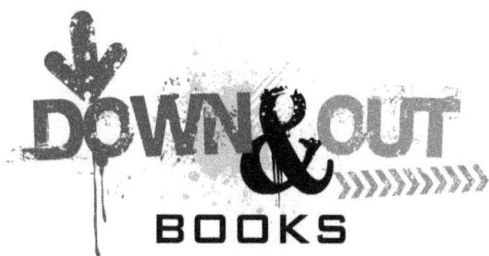

On the following pages are a few
more great titles from the
Down & Out Books publishing family.

For a complete list of books and to
sign up for our newsletter,
go to DownAndOutBooks.com.

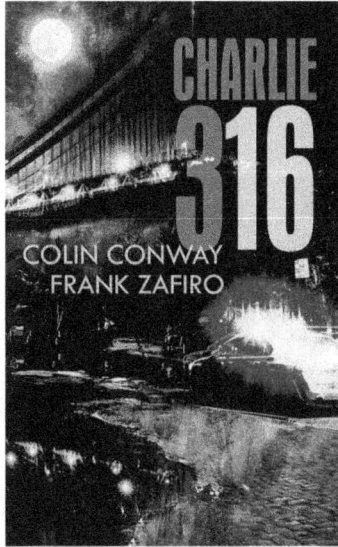

Charlie 316
Colin Conway and Frank Zafiro

Down & Out Books
June 2018
978-1-948235-68-6

A criminal/political thriller surrounding the investigation of an officer-involved shooting.

Surviving an ambush by killing the suspected shooter doesn't guarantee Officer Tyler Garrett safety, especially when the suspect was shot in the back and his gun has disappeared.

Will the department and city hall close ranks and protect Garrett? Or will they step back and allow him to twist in the wind?

The Ornery Gene
Warren C. Embree

Down & Out Books
April 2019
978-1-64396-012-8

When itinerant ranch hand Buck Ellison took a job with Sarah Watkins at her ranch in the Sandhills of Nebraska, he thought he had found the place where he could park his pickup, leave the past behind, and never move again.

On a rainy July night, a dead man found at the south end of Sarah's ranch forces him to become a reluctant detective, delving into the business of cattle breeding for rodeos and digging up events from his past that are linked to the circumstances surrounding the murder of Sam Danielson.

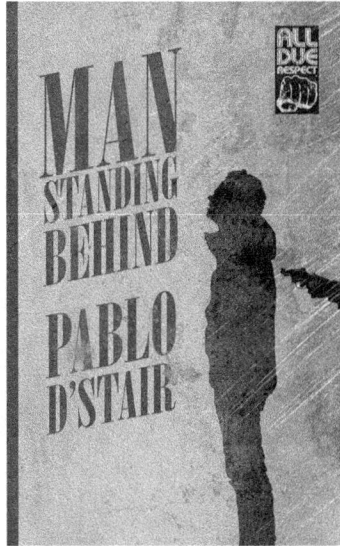

Man Standing Behind
Pablo D'Stair

All Due Respect, an imprint of
Down & Out Books
May 2019
978-1-64396-035-7

Leaving work on a nondescript evening, Roger is held up at gunpoint when he stops at a cash machine. But robbery isn't on the gunman's mind...Roger is told simply to walk.

The gunman takes him on a macabre odyssey—from city pubs to suburban neighborhoods to isolated homes in the country—and as the night presses on, a seemingly not-so-random body count grows around him.

A man caught in the roils of a mortal circumstance having nothing to do with his own life. Is he a witness, a victim...or something altogether worse?

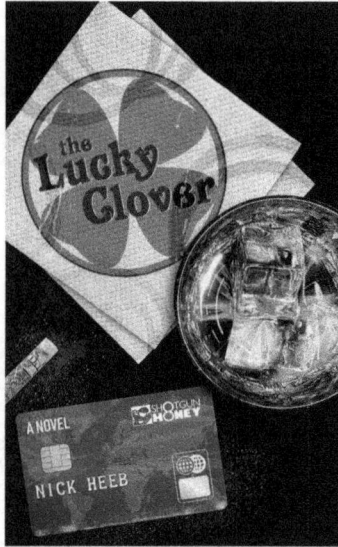

The Lucky Clover
Nick Heeb

Shotgun Honey, an imprint of
Down & Out Books
978-1-948235-69-3

When the Narrator returns to his old haunt, The Lucky Clover, he is looking to forget and recover from his past life's miseries and humiliations by drinking with good friends.

He soon discovers the people closest to him had no interest in his honest intentions, and that violence is the only language spoken in this sparse and hard country he calls home.

www.ingramcontent.com/pod-product-compliance
Lightning Source LLC
Chambersburg PA
CBHW020252030426
42336CB00010B/721